EXPLORING SCIENCE

INVENTIONS & DISCOVERIES

AN AMAZING FACT FILE AND HANDS-ON PROJECT BOOK

With 13 easy experiments and over 270 exciting pictures

JOHN FARNDON

ARMADILLO

This edition is published by Armadillo, an imprint of Anness Publishing Ltd, 108 Great Russell Street, London WC1B 3NA; info@anness.com

www.annesspublishing.com; twitter: @Anness_Books

Anness Publishing has a picture agency outlet for images for publishing, promotions or advertising. Please visit our website www.practicalpictures.com for more information.

© Anness Publishing Ltd 2017

Publisher: Joanna Lorenz
Editor: Richard McGinlay
Special Photography: John Freeman
Illustrators: Julian Baker, Dave Bowyer, Peter Bull Art Studio, Stuart Carter, Jerry Fowler, Rob Sheffield, Catherine Ward/Simon Girling Associates

PICTURE CREDITS
b=bottom, t=top, m=middle, l=left, r=right
Alamy/World History Archive 52tl; Ancient Art and Architecture Ltd 12tr; Ann Ronan Picture Library 36tl, 36bl, 36br, 55tl; The Art Archive 10tr; Barnaby's Picture Library 16br; Bridgeman Art Library 20tl; Comstock 3tr, 3ml, 52bl, 53tl, 54tr, 55tr, 62bl; Corbis 8tl, 18bl, 28br, 39tr, 40tr, 40bl, 58tr; Dzudzuana Joint Excavation Team (Georgia-USA-Israel)/Dr E Kvavadze 8bl; ET Archive 3mr, 8br, 18tl, 25bl, 54br; HighestBridges.com/Jon Fether, Jesus Catalan and Eric Sakowski 23br; Hulton Getty Picture Library 40br, 50br, 56t; Hutchison Picture Library/Robert Francis 10br; iStock/AzmanL 59ml, /TheBroker 37bl, /Duncan1890 33tl, /Luke Miller 13ml, /Rzelich 53bl, /Typhoonski 34br; Mary Evans Picture Library 46tr, 47tl; National Maritime Museum 28bl, 29tl, 29tr; PhotoDisc 42ml, 42bl; Science and Society Picture Library 1, 2br, 9tl, 9tr, 16tl, 17tl, 19m, 28tl, 29bl, 35bl, 40mr, 46bl, 46br, 47ml, 47mr, 47br, 48tl, 56b, 57tr, 57ml, 58bl, 58br; Science Photo Library 59tr; Shutterstock/ABB Photo 34tl, /Chombosan 37br, /Elenarts 24mr, /Eduardo Estellez 22tr, /Everett Art 24bl, /Everett Historical 9bl, /Liubov Fediashova 44br, /Olga Gavrilova 23tl, /Len Green 23tr, /Dmitry Kalinovsky 9br, /Zern Liew 22bl, /Mandritoiu 23m, /Morphart Creation 52br, /Nilovsergey 3tl, /Nilovsergey 19tr, /Slavoljub Pantelic 41b, /Dario Lo Presti 31t, /Ruzanna 5bl, /Scanrail1 3br, /Scanrail1 19br, /Science Photo 17bl, /Richard Semik 12br, /DrSerg 59mr, /SpeedKingz 51mr, /Tinxi 59br, /G Tipene 13b, /Sergiy Zavgorodny 31mr; Tony Stone Images 14tr; TRH Pictures 3b, 31b, 41tr, 45ml; Wikimedia Commons/Chris Allen 38bl, /Staff Sgt Aaron Allmon II 41ml, /José-Manuel Benito Álvarez 5tl, /Anders 55br (with iPhone from Carl Berkeley), /Aronagust 39tl, /Avda 37mr, /Pete Brown 53tr, /Chris Burks 57mr, /Didier Descouens 4tr, /DimiTVP 39b, /PTG Dudva 33br, /Fastfission 44tl, /Julian Herzog 39mr, /Ji-Elle 30br, /D-Kuru 57br, /Hugh Llewelyn 33mr, /NASA 44bl, 45tl, 45mr, 55bl, /National Oceanic and Atmospheric Administration 31ml, /Public Domain 17mr, 18br, 19bl, 25tr, 25bl, 33ml, 35tl, 35br, 38br, 47tr, 50tr, 50bl, 51tl, 51tr, 51ml, 54ml, 54bl, /Roby 38tl, /Ronrosano 45br, /David Shankbone 35tr, /Colin Smith 30tl, /Softeis 37tl, /Tamorlan 32tr, /Wellcome Images 30bl, 49bl.

PUBLISHER'S NOTE

Manufacturer: Anness Publishing Ltd, 108 Great Russell Street, London WC1B 3NA, England
For Product Tracking go to: www.annesspublishing.com/tracking
Batch: 7400-23844-1127

CONTENTS

THE FIRST INVENTIONS

HUMANS are a very inventive bunch. Every day, each one of us thinks of some new way to do something – or avoid doing something! You might invent a new way to fold your clothes, or tell a joke. Most inventions are quickly forgotten. But some of them are so clever and so useful that lots of people start to use them. Some even change the world.

Some of the greatest inventions were thought up by our human-like ancestors long before we humans even existed. Experts have found stone tools in Ethiopia that they believe could be over 2.6 million years old! Ancestors of ours learned how to make fires, and also how to cook, at least 1 million years ago. Half a million years or so ago, our ancestors invented huts and spears as well. We humans appeared just 200,000 years ago, and have been even more inventive. Long before anyone knew how to write it all down, humans had invented clothing and musical instruments, bows and arrows, pottery, and the wheel.

Ancient axes
A hand axe is a stone that fits snugly in your hand, with one edge chipped away to form a sharp blade. With a blade, our ancestors could cut up meat, or animal skins to make clothes, or branches to make shelters. Hand axes were so effective that they were used for over 2 million years, far longer than any other invention.

Stone-tipped spear
The invention of the spear was what turned humans into hunters, who could track down and kill large animals. The first wooden spears date back at least half a million years. Then about 200,000 years ago, someone had the idea of attaching a stone blade to the head. That not only gave a stronger, sharper tip, but meant the spear could be thrown from a safe distance.

The first fires
Fires can start naturally when, for instance, lightning strikes. But over a million years ago, our ancestors *Homo erectus* discovered that they could light their own small, controlled fires by using embers from a natural fire. Fire allowed them to cook and eat meat and tough vegetables. It kept them warm, gave them light at night, and also provided them with protection against wild animals.

The Geisenklösterle flute

No one knows when people first started making music or why. Experts think it was a way of keeping people together. The oldest known musical instrument is a flute made from a swan bone pierced with holes. It was found in the Geisenklösterle cave in Swabia in Germany. It is between 42,000 and 43,000 years old.

Bow and arrow

The bow and arrow made humans even more effective hunters than the spear did. A skilled archer could kill or wound a running animal from a great distance. The first bows and arrows may have been used in Africa 71,000 years ago. The oldest known bow was found preserved in the mud of Holmegaard Swamp in Denmark. It is 11,000 years old.

Doing cart wheels

When humans lived by hunting and gathering food, they travelled light. But around 12,000 years ago, they settled down to farm and began to live in cities. They needed ways to move farm produce and building materials around in bulk. The solution was the wheeled cart. Carts with solid wooden wheels appeared about the same time, 5,000–6,000 years ago, in Sumeria in the Near East (shown here), in the Caucasus mountains and in Central Europe.

Grinding wheel

Before you can cook and eat the seeds of wheat and other cereal crops, you need to grind them down into flour. Early farmers probably did this by painstakingly crushing seeds under a heavy stone or 'quern'. Then someone discovered that if you set two querns together, you could just turn one to grind the seeds between them. Flat disc-shaped querns called millstones worked even better. Until recently, all flour was made with millstones like this.

Pottering around

Besides the cart wheel and the grinding wheel, there was one other key wheel invention from ancient times: the potter's wheel. This dates back about 6,500 years. Previously, pots had been shaped by carefully coiling sausages of clay up in a spiral. But a lump of clay could be drawn up quickly and easily by hand on a spinning stone, the potter's wheel, into a round pot.

MAKING FIRE

T HE oldest known signs of a fire used by our ancestors come from Wonderwerk Cave in South Africa, and date back more than 1 million years. At first, our ancestors did not know how to make fire, but found embers left over from natural forest fires. They took care to keep their campfires alight, and carried hot embers wrapped in leaves to start new fires. Eventually, they learned that they could light a fire with a spark created by striking hard stones together.

Later, they found they could make fire with the heat given off by rubbing two dry sticks together. First, they spun a thin stick very fast between their hands against a notch in a piece of wood filled with tinder (flammable material, such as dry grass). This is called a hand drill. Then about 6,000 years ago, it was discovered that you can spin the stick much faster and easier with a bow drill.

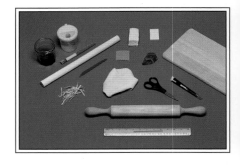

BOW DRILL

You will need: *thick piece of dowel (25cm/10in long), craft knife, sandpaper, wood stain, paintbrush, water pot, balsa wood (8 x 8cm/3⅛ x 3⅛in), modelling tool, self-hardening clay, rolling pin, cutting board, scissors, chamois leather, raffia or straw.*

Forest firelighting

Native tribes in the Amazon rainforest such as the Yanomami people still use a hand drill to start fires. It's a very skilled task. Spinning the stick is not easy and you have to add just the right tinder to catch the heat. But it's such a simple method technologically that you can do it anywhere there's wood.

The first match

One way early people made fire was to put dry grass on a stick called a hearth. Then they rubbed another stick against the hearth to make a spark and set the grass alight.

hearth

1 Shape one end of the piece of thick dowel into a point with a craft knife. The blade of the knife should always angle away from your body when you cut the wood.

2 Sand down the stick and apply a coat of wood stain. Cut out the balsa wood base into a shape roughly like the one shown above. Paint the base with wood stain. Leave it to dry.

3 Use a modelling tool to gouge a small hole in the middle of the balsa wood base. The sharpened end of the piece of dowel should fit into this hole.

4 Roll out a piece of clay. Cut out a bone shape with a rounded end. Make a hole in each end of the bone and smooth the sides with your fingers. Let the bone shape dry.

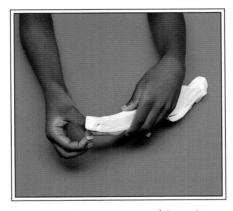

5 Use scissors to cut a thin strip of chamois leather twice as long as the bone. This will be the thong used to twist the bow drill. Tie the strip to one end of the bone.

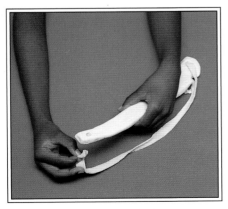

6 Thread the strip of chamois leather through the other hole. Tie a knot at the end to secure it. Now the bow piece is ready to be used with the drill you have made.

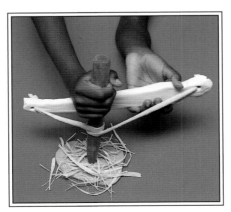

7 Scatter raffia or straw around the balsa wood base. Wrap the leather thong around the drill piece and place the pointed end of the drill in the hole on the base.

If you like, add a wood handle to the base to help you hold it. The drill you have made will not light real fires, but it shows how ancient people spun a drill to make fire.

WEAVING

Ancient silk
The exquisite beauty of ancient Chinese silk is still very clear in this gorgeous banner found perfectly preserved in a Chinese emperor's tomb at Mawangdui from 1,800 years ago.

PEOPLE began wearing animal skins about 170,000 years ago, maybe to protect their bodies from the sun, or from the cold. Then about 40,000 years ago, they started making proper clothes by sewing skins together with a needle and thread. But the great breakthrough was finding out how to make cloth by weaving. To weave cloth, two sets of thin fibres are interlaced at right angles, over and under each other, using a device called a loom. The threads might be twisted plant fibres such as flax (for making linen) and cotton, or sheep's wool.

For thousands of years, cloth was made by people working at home using spinning wheels to make the threads, and hand looms to weave it. Then in the 18th century, special spinning and weaving machines were invented in Britain. Powered by water wheels and then by steam engines, these machines were installed in the first great factories to make cloth on a huge scale. In the 1900s, artificial threads such as nylon were invented that allowed new kinds of cloth to be made.

Old weave
The oldest known pieces of cloth were found in the very ancient town of Çatalhöyük in Turkey and date back 8,000 years, but weaving may have been invented much earlier. A few years ago, researchers found neatly cut flax fibres in a cave at Dzudzuana in the Republic of Georgia. The fibres are over 30,000 years old and dyed in various colours, but it is not certain if they were used for weaving.

Silken secret
About 6,000 years ago, the Chinese discovered silk. This is a beautiful cloth woven from the silken threads that silk-moth caterpillars make their cocoons from. Chinese silk was so miraculously beautiful that the Emperors of Rome had it brought to them across Asia along the legendary Silk Road. But for a long time, the Chinese kept how it was made a secret.

Spin me a yarn

In ancient times, the thread used for weaving, known as yarn, was made by spinning fibres together by hand on a stick called a distaff. Then about 1,500 years ago in India, the spinning wheel was invented. The wheel was turned by a pedal, leaving both of the spinster's hands free to feed in the fibres.

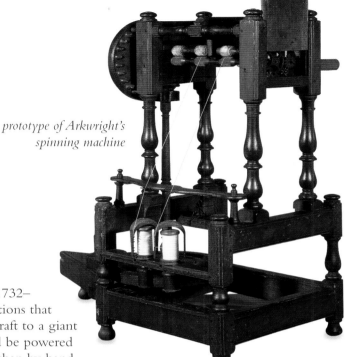

prototype of Arkwright's spinning machine

1300s spinning wheel

Water power

The 'water frame' invented by Richard Arkwright (1732–1792) in 1769 was one of many 18th-century inventions that transformed cloth-making in Britain from a home craft to a giant industry. It was called a water frame because it could be powered by a water wheel to spin cotton much, much faster than by hand. Water-powered looms soon followed.

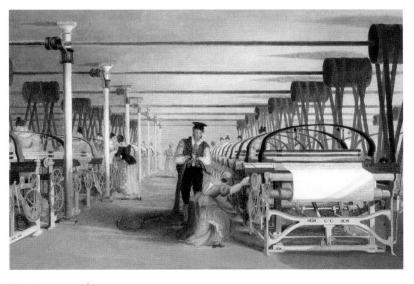

Factory setting

Up until the 18th century, most things, including cloth, were made by skilled craftsmen and women at their homes or in workshops. But in 1771, Richard Arkwright installed dozens of machines in the first proper factory to make cloth on a large scale. Early factories were called mills because they were powered by water wheels. But soon water wheels were replaced by steam engines.

Slinky and sporty

Olympic racers wear suits of a silky smooth and stretchy material called lycra. This is a special cloth made entirely from manmade fibres. The fibres are created by forcing a plastic-like material called a polymer through a tiny hole.

BACKSTRAP LOOM

I N ANCIENT times, homes were not just places to eat and sleep. They were workplaces, too. Weaving was a skill learned by all women in Mesoamerica (Mexico and Central America) and in the Andean region, for instance, and they spent long hours spinning thread and weaving it into cloth. As well as making tunics, cloaks and other items of clothing for the family, they had to give some to the rulers as a form of tax payment. Cotton was spun and woven into textiles for the wealthiest citizens of Mesoamerica. Peasants wore clothes made from the woven fibres of local plants such as the yucca and maguey.

Yarn was dyed before it was woven. Most dyes originated from the flowers, fruits and leaves of plants, but some were extracted from shellfish and insects such as the cochineal beetle − a tiny insect that lives on cactus plants.

Skirts, tunics and cloaks
A wealthy Aztec couple sit by the fire, while their hostess cooks a meal. Both of the women are wearing long skirts. The bright embroidery on their tunics is a sign of high rank.

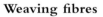

Weaving fibres
Threads spun from plant fibres were woven into cloth on backstrap looms such as this one. Rough fibres from the yucca and cactus plants made coarse cloth. The wealthy had silky textiles.

Down Mexico way
These Mexican women are wearing warm woollen ponchos in bright colours that would also have appealed to their ancestors.

MESOAMERICAN LOOM

You will need: *two pieces of thick dowel about 70cm/27½in long, brown water-based paint, paintbrush, water pot, string, scissors, thick card, pencil, ruler, masking tape, yellow and red wool, needle.*

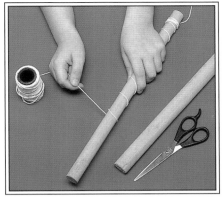

1 Paint the pieces of dowel brown. Leave them to dry. Tie a length of string to each length of dowel and wind it around. Leave a length of string loose at each end.

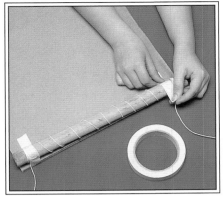

2 Cut a piece of thick card about 100 x 70cm/40 x 28in. This is a temporary base. Lightly fix the stringed dowel at the 70cm/28in sides of the base using masking tape.

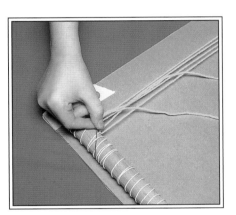

3 Thread the yellow wool through the string loops using the needle. Pull through to the other end, as shown above. Try to keep the yellow wool taut.

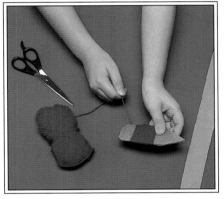

4 Cut a 30 x 3.5cm/12 x 1½in piece of thick card. Now cut a smaller rectangle of card with one pointed end, as shown above. Wind the red wool tightly around it.

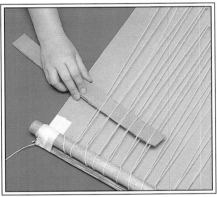

5 Slide the long card rectangle through every second thread. This 'shed rod' is turned on its side to lift the threads. Then tie one end of the red wool to the yellow wool.

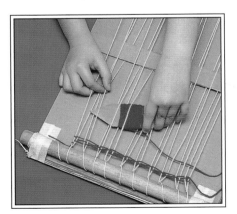

6 Turn the rod on its side to lift the threads and feed the red wool through the loom. Then, with the rod flat, thread the red wool back through alternate yellow threads.

To continue weaving, take the loom off the card base. Tie the loose string around your waist. Attach the other end of the loom to a post or tree with the string. Lean back to keep the long warp threads evenly taut.

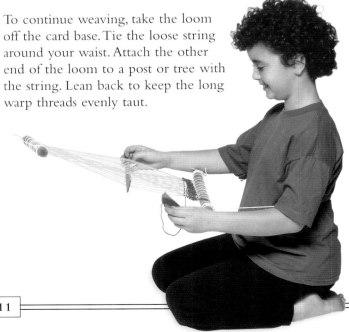

METALS

For millions of years, in what is called the Stone Age, the only tools were sharpened stones, sticks and old bones. Then, about 10,000 years ago, we discovered metals. Metals can be heated and then moulded or beaten into pretty much any shape.

The first metal objects were ornaments of soft copper and gold, found in the ground in tiny amounts. Then, 6,000–7,000 years ago, it was realized that you can get metals in much larger amounts by melting it out of rocks called ores and, also, that by adding a little tin and arsenic to copper you can create bronze. Bronze was tough enough to make the first metal tools and weapons – and so move the world into what is called the Bronze Age. Only the rich could afford bronze, though, and the big breakthrough was the discovery of iron 4,500 years or so ago by metalworkers in Anatolia (Turkey), launching the Iron Age. Iron was so cheap and plentiful that soon more or less everybody was using iron tools and weapons.

The coming of bronze

Bronze could be used to make axes and spearheads. But unlike stone, it was also possible to make the first swords and suits of armour. No one knows exactly where bronze was first discovered, and the Bronze Age started at different times in different parts of the world. Bronze-making began in the Middle East 6,000 years ago, and then spread west across Europe and east into India. It was the world's first major industry, and international trade developed as metalworkers looked for ores in mines as far apart as Timna in Egypt and Mount Gabriel in Ireland.

The Iron Age

The discovery of iron-making changed the world. Iron ores are so plentiful that iron could be used to make everything from swords for ordinary soldiers to ploughshares and nails. And soon iron-makers found that by including carbon from the charcoal they used to melt the iron, they could make tough steel – which is still the best tool- and blade-making metal of all.

The iron revolution

In the 18th century in England, iron-makers learned how to make cast iron on a huge scale using coke to fire very hot 'blast' furnaces. For the first time, iron could be used to build things. The famous Iron Bridge in Shropshire (above), constructed between 1777 and 1781, was just the first of many fantastic iron structures – from the Forth Rail Bridge to the Eiffel Tower, as well as railways.

Steel yourself

Blast furnaces could make iron on an industrial scale, but not steel. Then in 1856, Sir Henry Bessemer invented the Bessemer converter to transform huge amounts of iron into steel. Air is blown into molten iron inside the converter to take away any impurities, and then the right additives are put in to create strong steel for use in a vast range of items, from ships to saucepans.

Aluminium extraction

In the late 1800s, the electrolytic cell was invented as a way of using electricity to extract aluminium from bauxite ore. The metal is separated using electricity, a process known as electrolysis (right). Aluminium is cheap, light and strong, and is used for making everything from aircraft to computer bodies (below).

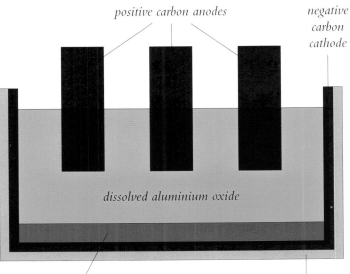

positive carbon anodes

negative carbon cathode

dissolved aluminium oxide

molten aluminium collects at bottom

steel container

Tough titanium

Titanium was discovered in Cornwall, Great Britain, by William Gregor in 1791, but it wasn't until the 1950s that it began to be widely used. It's expensive, but it is incredibly tough and light, which is why it is a good metal for high-performance aircraft. Each Airbus A380 uses 77 tons of titanium in its body and jet engines.

CREATING CHEMICALS

OVER the last century or so, scientists have created many new substances including plastics such as polythene and PVC (polyvinyl chloride), composite materials such as Kevlar, and medicines such as ibuprofen. These new substances are mostly created by mixing natural ones that react to each other in what are called chemical reactions. There are three main ways in which scientists can provoke chemical reactions: passing electricity through things (electrolysis), heating them or mixing them together.

The following experiments show each of these kinds of chemical reaction. In the first project, electricity breaks down salty water to make chlorine, which is used as a disinfectant to keep swimming pools clean. In the second project, you heat sugar, which is made from carbon, hydrogen and oxygen to create pure carbon. The third shows how to make the gas used in some fire extinguishers. This gas is carbon dioxide and is made by mixing bicarbonate of soda and vinegar together.

Measuring up
In a laboratory, this scientist is carefully measuring the exact amount of chemicals to add to a test tube in which the experiment will take place. In science, accuracy is very important.

ELECTROLYSIS

You will need: *screwdriver, battery (4–6 volts), bulb and holder, wire, 2 paper clips, glass jar, water, salt.*

WARNING!
Please take care when using electrical equipment. Always have an adult present.

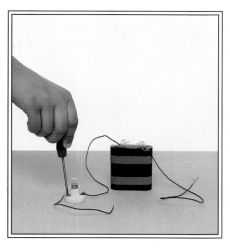

1 Connect the battery and bulb holder with wires as shown here. Remove 1cm/½in of insulation from each end. Use the paper clips to join the wires to the battery.

2 Stir salt into a jar of water until no more dissolves. Dip the two bare wire ends into the mixture and hold them 1cm/½in apart. Look for bubbles forming around them.

3 The bulb should light up to show that electricity is passing through. Carefully sniff the jar from 20cm/8in away. The smell is like swimming pools.

HEAT CHANGES

You will need: *old pan that no one needs any more (see warning below), teaspoon, sugar, cooker.*

1 Make sure the pan is completely dry. Spread one teaspoonful of sugar across the bottom of the pan. Aim for a thin layer a few millimetres or ⅛in thick.

2 Place the pan on a cooker set to low heat. After a few minutes, the sugar will start to melt and produce a brown treacly liquid. You may see a few wisps of steam.

WARNING!
Be sure to get permission before using the pan, as this project will probably ruin it!

3 The sugar starts to bubble as it breaks down and gives off steam. If you carry on heating, the brown sticky liquid will change to solid black carbon.

MIXING THINGS

You will need: *teaspoon, bicarbonate of soda (baking soda), glass bowl, spirit vinegar, matches.*

1 Place three heaped spoonfuls of bicarbonate of soda in the bowl. Cooks often add this white powder to vegetables such as peas and carrots. It helps to keep their natural colour.

2 Pour vinegar into the bowl. As the liquid mixes with the white powdery bicarbonate of soda, a chemical reaction happens. The mixture bubbles as a gas is given off.

3 Ask an adult to light a match and lower the flame into the bowl. The chemical reaction has made a gas called carbon dioxide. The flame goes out when it meets the gas.

FIGHTING ILLNESS

early stethoscopes

DOCTORS today know a lot about the human body and have many treatments, drugs and machines to help them cure illnesses. The first specialist doctors appeared in the time of Ancient Egypt nearly 5,000 years ago. Since then, many doctors and scientists have contributed to the growth of our medical knowledge. In the 1530s, for instance, Italian doctor Andreas Vesalius realized that the only way to find out about human anatomy was to cut open dead bodies. Then in the early 1600s, William Harvey showed that blood is pumped round and round the body by the heart (blood circulation). In 1796, English doctor Edward Jenner took an old Chinese idea, and demonstrated how you can stop people getting ill from diseases by priming the body's natural defences (vaccination).

In the mid-1800s, doctors such as Ignaz Semmelweis and Joseph Lister showed how hygiene is vital for stopping the spread of diseases. Then in 1865, French scientist Louis Pasteur proved that most diseases are caused by microscopic germs such as bacteria, and in the 1920s, British doctor Alexander Fleming discovered penicillin, the first 'antibiotic' drug known to kill bacteria.

What's going on inside?

In 1816, French doctor René Laënnec had the idea of listening to a patient's chest to detect problems with the heart and lungs through a tube called a stethoscope. Doctors still use stethoscopes, but nowadays they are also helped by electronic scanners such as CT scanners and MRI scanners, which use radiation to take pictures inside the body.

FACT BOX

• In 1829, Dr James Blundell carried out the first successful human-to-human blood transfusion, by injecting into a patient blood that had been taken from the patient's husband.

• Dr Willem Kolff invented the first artificial kidney machine in 1943. Like a kidney, the machine removes poisons from a person's bloodstream. People whose kidneys are too damaged to work use this machine.

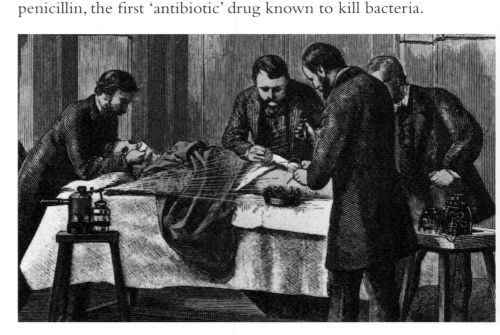

Keeping clean

Before the 1860s, many people died from infection after surgery because no one knew the dangers of germs infecting open wounds. Then British surgeon Joseph Lister introduced 'antiseptic' surgery. He made sure that hands, knives and every surface were thoroughly washed with germ-killing carbolic sprays. Now surgeons wear gloves, too, and also masks to stop germs spreading through the air.

Painkillers

If you've got a bad headache, or some other pain, you might well take a simple painkilling tablet. But until the invention of aspirin there were no pills like this. People had noticed long ago that chewing on the bark of willow trees helped to relieve pain. But it was only in the 1890s that the Bayer chemical company found that the key ingredient in willow could be used to make a simple powder they called aspirin.

ether inhaler

You won't feel a thing

Nowadays, surgeons send patients entirely to sleep with drugs called general anaesthetics before they perform a major operation such as a heart transplant. General anaesthetics were used for the first time in 1846, when American dentist William Morton sent a patient to sleep with vapours from the chemical ether while he pulled a tooth out. Ether inhalers like the one shown here were soon widely used for operations. Now other chemicals are used.

Vaccination

The Chinese discovered long ago you can protect people against smallpox by deliberately infecting them. But there was a risk that you might just die of the disease. Then British doctor Edward Jenner noticed that milkmaids who had caught the mild disease cowpox from their cows never got smallpox. He wondered whether cowpox germs might protect against smallpox without the risks. So in 1796 he injected cowpox pus into eight-year-old James Phipps. This cartoon from the time makes fun of fears of what might happen if you are injected with cowpox! Luckily for James Phipps, the idea worked. Indeed, it worked so well that by 1979 smallpox was entirely eradicated from the world.

Medicine from mould

In 1928, Alexander Fleming went away on holiday while trying to grow germs in dishes in his laboratory. When he came back, he found that the germs had died where a mould had grown — and realized the mould contained a natural germ-killing substance he called penicillin. Howard Florey and Ernst Chain turned Fleming's penicillin into the first antibiotic medicine and would save around 200 million lives.

MARKING TIME

Shadow of time
This Ancient Roman sundial is cut in the shape of a shell from a block of marble. Sundials were made in many shapes and sizes. People could judge the time by watching as the shadow cast by the sun moved from one line to another.

For many years, people knew pretty well what time of day it was just by looking at where the sun was in the sky. Indeed, very early timepieces were sundials, which date back at least 3,500 years to the time of Ancient Egypt. But sundials don't work at night or in cloudy weather, and they can't show intervals of time passing, such as hours, minutes and seconds. This is why we have clocks.

The first mechanical clock in the world was invented in China in AD725 by Yi Xing and Liang Lingzan, and by the 1300s there were clocks in Europe, too. Since then, clocks have become ever more accurate, and generally smaller. Early mechanical clocks used cogs and weights to turn the hands. Replacing weights with springs allowed clocks to be much smaller and more portable, enabling the first pocket watch to be made in 1524. Spring-driven timepieces are wound up with a key. Now watches and other timekeepers are electronic and very accurate. The most accurate clocks of all, though, are atomic, and can measure a billion billionth of a second.

On the hour
This clock in St Mark's Square in Venice dates from the late 1400s. At that time, only major churches would have had such a large and expensive mechanism as a clock. Churches needed to mark out the 'hours', the times of day when religious people were meant to pray.

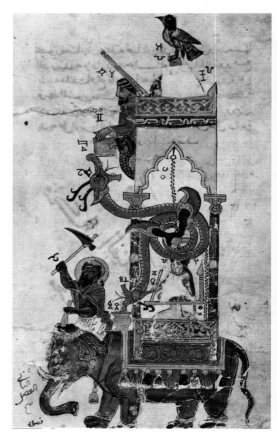

Water clock
Long before mechanical clocks, water clocks showed time passing as water flowed slowly and steadily from a tank. The most ingenious water clocks were made in the 13th century by Al-Jazari in Anatolia, including his 'elephant clock' in which a model man and bird moved about automatically as the hour passed.

Pendulum clock

A pendulum clock is a clock that uses a pendulum, a swinging weight, for timekeeping. The advantage of a pendulum is that it swings back and forth in a precise time interval. From its invention in 1656 by Christiaan Huygens until the 1930s, the pendulum clock was the most precise timekeeper in the world. Pendulum clocks must be kept still in order to work properly. Any movement would affect the motion of the pendulum, causing inaccuracies, so other mechanisms must be used in portable timepieces, such as pocket watches.

Precious time

A pocket watch was expensive to make and owned only by those with money to spend. A metal case protected the watch from bumps and thumps. This watch was made in 1759. Its many tiny wheels and cogs would have taken months for a skilled watchmaker to make and fit together.

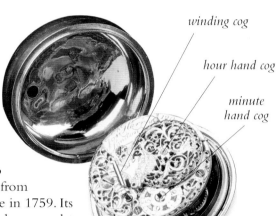

winding cog

hour hand cog

minute hand cog

Electronic time

Very few clocks use weights or springs to keep time now. Instead, clocks like the one in a smartphone or a smart watch are kept in time by the regular vibrations of tiny crystals. These create an electric signal to generate the change in the time displayed. They keep updating by synchronizing over the internet with highly accurate clocks.

Atomic time

In 1955, Louis Essen and Jack Parry built the world's first atomic clock, using rapid regular changes in energy inside caesium atoms. Atomic clocks are the world's most accurate clocks, losing just one second every 15 billion years! A network of atomic clocks such as the NIST F2 in the USA now keep time for the whole world to set their clocks by.

IT'S EXPERIMENT TIME

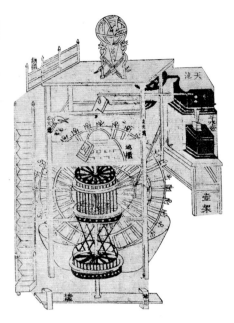

Water timer
This Chinese water clock was built in 1088. Water trickles into tiny buckets fixed to the outside of a large wheel. As each bucket fills up, the wheel clicks round to the next empty bucket. Each bucket empties as it reaches the lowest position. The position of the wheel indicates the time.

I N THESE projects, you can make a water clock (right) and a pendulum clock (below). Water clocks may be the world's oldest timepieces. The Ancient Egyptians were using them at least 3,000 years ago, and the Chinese maybe 6,000 years ago. They keep time using the small but steady flow of water out of a bowl or into another through a narrow hole. The level of water in the bowl indicates the time that has passed. However, even the best water clocks can only show minutes passing, not seconds.

Then in 1602, the Italian scientist Galileo Galilei noticed something interesting about pendulums – heavy weights that swing on a rope or chain. Once swinging, they always take exactly the same time to swing to and fro. He realized that a pendulum might be used to keep time in a clock, with each swing of the pendulum letting the hands move round at regular intervals. In 1649, Galileo's son Vincenzio tried to make a pendulum clock. But the first working pendulum clock was made by Dutch scientist Christiaan Huygens in 1656. Pendulum clocks were the first clocks able to measure seconds.

MAKE A PENDULUM

You will need: *modelling clay, string, stopwatch.*

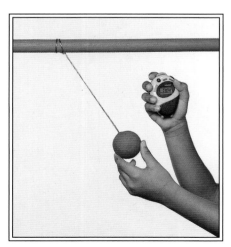

1 Roll some clay to make a ball 4cm/1½in across. Use string to hang it 30cm/12in below a support. Pull the ball out to the position shown. Let go and time ten complete swings.

2 Repeat the experiment. This time, use a larger, heavier ball with the same bit of string. You will find that the time for ten swings is the same despite the heavier ball.

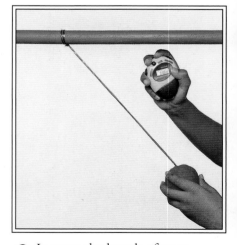

3 Increase the length of your pendulum by hanging the ball from a longer piece of string. You will find that the pendulum swings more slowly than before.

MAKE A WATER CLOCK

You will need: *bradawl or awl, aluminium pie dish, drinking straw, large plastic tumbler, scissors, water, marker pen.*

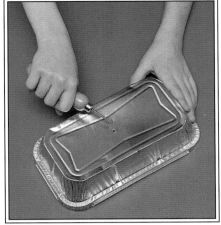

1 Use the bradawl to make a small hole in the bottom of the pie dish. The smaller the hole, the longer your water clock will run.

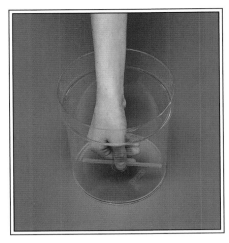

2 Place the straw in the plastic tumbler. It will act as a pointer as the water level rises. Cut the straw with a pair of scissors if it is too long.

3 Place the pie dish on top of the plastic tumbler. Make sure the hole in the pie dish is over the middle of the tumbler.

4 Pour water into the pie dish. Keep adding water until the dish is full. As soon as water starts to fall into the tumbler, note the time on your watch.

5 After 10 minutes, use the pen to mark the water level on the side of the tumbler. As the water drips into the tumbler, mark the level at 10-minute intervals.

You can use your pie-dish water clock to time your eggs for breakfast.

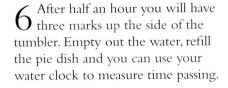

6 After half an hour you will have three marks up the side of the tumbler. Empty out the water, refill the pie dish and you can use your water clock to measure time passing.

BUILDING BRIDGES

PEOPLE learned how to build bridges from stone over 3,000 years ago. The secret was to arrange the stones in an arch. If the stones are narrower at the bottom, they push down against each other as weight is put on them. That makes an arch very strong. Stone arches were the main kind of bridge for thousands of years. The Romans built arch bridges that are still standing today. In the 18th century, iron became available in bulk, and engineers made arch bridges from iron, like the famous Iron Bridge (see page 12). But they soon realized iron could be used for bridges in different ways. A road or railway could be carried across a river suspended from iron chains, for instance. Suspension bridges like the Menai Bridge of 1826 revolutionized bridge-building. Suspension bridges can be flung across vast spans, high enough for even tall ships to pass under them. Since then, suspension bridges have become ever more ambitious, and have been joined by other kinds of metal bridge, such as cantilever and cable-stayed types.

Spanning Spain
By combining multiple arches with tall pillars, the Romans were able to span wide valleys, as with the spectacular Alcantara Bridge in Spain, built between AD104 and 106.

arch bridge

beam bridge

truss bridge

cantilever truss bridge

suspension bridge

cable-stayed bridge

Types of bridge
One of the oldest and simplest types of bridge is the arch, which is carried by a curving arch or arches of stone, concrete or steel. Beam bridges are even simpler and older, supported by rigid beams, typically iron girders. Truss bridges rely on a framework made up of triangles of steel. Cantilever bridges project out from strong anchor points either side to meet in the middle. A cantilever truss uses a truss frame in the same way, projecting trusses out from an anchor point. With suspension bridges, the bridge deck is held up by wires running down from strong cables suspended between two towers. In cable-stayed bridges, the cables that hold the deck are attached directly to the towers.

Shopping bridge

In the Middle Ages, bridges were often packed with shops, like the famous Ponte Vecchio ('old bridge') in Florence, Italy, built in 1345. It was originally famous for its butchers. Now the shops are jewellers and souvenir sellers.

High Menai

Rope suspension bridges had often been built before. But the metal chain suspension bridge built in 1826 over the Menai Strait in Wales by engineer Thomas Telford changed bridge-building forever. Telford's Menai Bridge, which many said could never be built, carried a single 176m/577ft span over 30m/100ft high, allowing tall ships to glide underneath in full sail.

Brooklyn Bridge

When it was opened in 1883, New York's Brooklyn Bridge, designed by John and Washington Roebling, was the biggest bridge in the world, with a main span over 500m/1,600ft long.

High wire act

The spectacular 565m/1,850ft high Beipanjiang Bridge Duge in China is the highest ever bridge. It is a cable-stayed bridge in which the bridge span is held up by wires tied to towers at either side. The Beipan River has more high bridges than any other river in the world.

TAKING TO THE SEA

OUR ancestors may have made boats to sail across the sea 130,000 years ago. The oldest boat ever found is a 10,000 year-old canoe scooped out from a log, which was preserved in the mud at Pesse in the Netherlands. But people at this time were already strapping logs together to make rafts, and setting up masts and sails to harness the power of the wind.

For 5,000 years, sailing boats were the best way of getting around the world. The first sails were square sails, which are simple but can only take a boat in much the same direction as the wind. Then 2,000 years ago triangular sails were developed which let a boat sail almost into the wind. Triangular sails helped Columbus to make the first voyage across the Atlantic to the West Indies in 1492. By the 1600s, huge sailing ships with many masts and dozens of sails were plying the oceans. But the age of sail came to an end in the 19th century, as the great sailing ships were superseded by vessels powered first by steam engines, then diesel turbines.

Reed all about it
By 5,000 years ago, the Egyptians were sailing up and down the River Nile in the first proper ships. Their ships' hulls were made of papyrus reeds bundled together. Later, they were skilfully built from planks of cedar wood, like the 4,500-year-old Khufu ship, the world's oldest ship, found intact inside the pyramid of Khufu.

Kings of the sea
1,200 years ago, the Vikings of Scandinavia were masters of the sea. Their ships were open boats with just a hull of overlapping planks (clinker-built), but they were very good at sea. Longships were slender and fast for raids. But wider, slower 'knarrs' were so stable that Viking settlers were able to sail right across to North America in about AD1000.

Oarsome power
Even 2,500 years ago, great sea battles were being fought between warring empires. But while sails were fine for cargo ships, warships called galleys had banks of oarsmen for extra speed and manoeuvrability. With their three rows of oars and a sturdy battering ram, Greek 'triremes' (three-rowers) were able to defeat the mighty Persian fleet at Salamis in 480BC.

Ships of the explorers

Square rig sails were fine for ships sailing in coastal waters. But in the 15th century, Portuguese sailors began to use fast, light ships called caravels, which had triangular 'lateen' sails. In caravels, European sailors could begin to explore far and wide across the ocean, knowing they could sail long distances quickly, and get home whatever the wind direction.

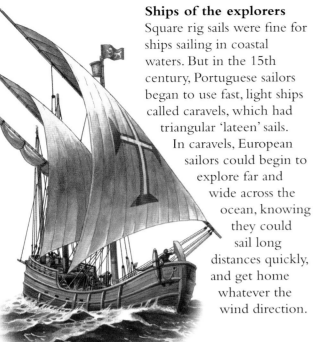

Men-o'-war

From the 16th century on, big ships began to trade around the world, each with two or three masts carrying three or more sails. On a long voyage, they could be many months at sea. Meanwhile, big, three-masted warships up to 60m/200ft long vied for control of the sea. They were armed with scores of cannons and called men-o'-war. In 1792, the English navy alone had 661 of these ships.

Steamed up

In summer 1819, the SS *Savannah* became the first steam-powered ship to cross the Atlantic Ocean. The steam engines turned paddle wheels either side of the ship. *Savannah* had sails as well, and only part of the journey was under steam. In 1838, the SS *Great Britain* and SS *Sirius* made the crossing entirely under steam.

Tea clippers

Sailing ships reached their peak in the 1860s, just before they were entirely eclipsed by steam power. 'Clippers' were streamlined ships with very tall masts and a vast area of sail. They could race 22,500km/14,000 miles from China to Europe in 99 days to get the season's tea to market first.

Turbine power

Just as the steam engine was coming into its own, it too was made to look old-fashioned by the steam turbine. The steam turbine uses steam not to push a piston to and fro but to whizz a fan blade round at high speed so that it generates electricity to power an electric motor. Launched in 1894, *Turbinia*, the first turbine-powered ship, was easily the fastest ship in the world, able to reach 64kmh/40mph.

VIKING LONGSHIP

THE Vikings were excellent seafarers, and were among the most skilful shipbuilders the world has ever seen. One of the most famous Viking vessels was the longship. It could be up to 23m/75ft in length. This long sailing ship was used for ocean voyages and warfare, and it was shallow enough to row up a river. The longship had an open deck without cabins or benches. The rowers sat on hide-covered sea chests that contained their possessions, weapons and food rations. A longship put to sea with a crew of about 30 fighting men.

A VESSEL FIT FOR A VIKING

You will need: *thick card, balsa wood strips and pole, pale and dark brown paper, plain paper, pencil, ruler, scissors, craft knife, acrylic paints (in black, brown and red), paintbrush, water pot, white glue and glue brush, masking tape, string.*

Templates
Ask an adult to cut out the card and balsa wood templates, following the measurements shown.

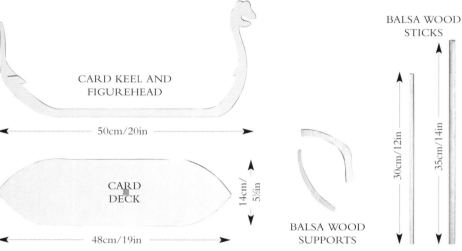

CARD KEEL AND FIGUREHEAD

50cm/20in

CARD DECK

14cm/5½in

48cm/19in

BALSA WOOD SUPPORTS

BALSA WOOD STICKS

30cm/12in

35cm/14in

2.5cm/1in   2.5cm/1in

BROWN PAPER STRIPS, VARYING (40–50cm/16–20in)

14cm/5½in

x3

CARD SUPPORTS

14cm/5½in

BALSA WOOD STRIPS x6

19cm/7½in

28cm/11in

PAPER SAIL

1 Paint the deck black on one side, brown on the other. Mark planks 5mm/¼in apart on the brown deck. Pierce a hole for the mast. Glue on three of the 14cm/5½in balsa strips.

2 Glue three 14cm/5½in balsa wood strips to the other side of the deck, matching them with the planks on the other side. Glue on the three card supports as crossbeams.

3 Carefully paint one side of the keel and figurehead template, using bright red acrylic paint. Leave it to dry, turn it over and paint the other side using the same colour.

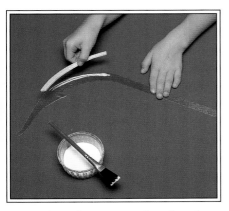

4 When the paint is dry, glue the two balsa wood supports either side of the curved parts of the keel, as shown. These will strengthen the keel and figurehead section.

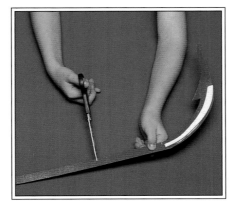

5 When the glue is dry, make three marks along the length of the keel, each one at a point that matches up to the crossbeams of the deck section. Use scissors to cut slots.

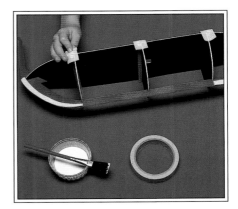

6 Slide the deck crossbeams into position on the keel slots, and glue them in place. Use masking tape to make sure the joins are firm while the glue is drying.

7 Use varying lengths of pale and dark brown paper strips for the planks, or 'strakes', along each side of the keel. Carefully glue each strip into position along each side.

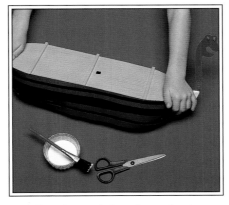

8 Continue gluing the strips into place. Alternate pale and dark brown strips to finish. Trim the excess off each strip as they get lower, so that they form a curve.

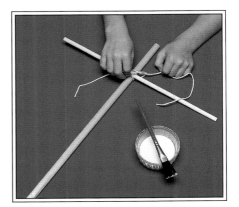

9 Make a mast using the 30cm/ 12in-long balsa wood and the 35cm/14in-long stick. Glue the two pieces firmly together and bind them with string, as shown above.

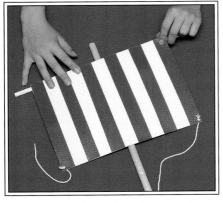

10 Paint the sail with red stripes. Glue the sail to the 30cm/ 12in cross beam. Attach string as rigging at the base of the sail. Add card eyes to the dragon figurehead.

The Vikings were major contributors to the shipbuilding technology of their day. Their methods spread through extensive contact with other cultures, and ships from the 11th and 12th centuries borrowed many of the longships' design features, despite the passing of many hundreds of years.

NAVIGATION

Star trek

Astrolabes were invented by the Ancient Greeks then developed by Muslim astronomers 1,300 years ago. They were used by sailors in Europe for navigation from the 1300s. The pointer or 'alidade' was aimed at a star, and its angle read on the dial.

IN ancient times, sailors had little to guide them once they were out of sight of land. The sun during the day and Pole Star at night could show you north and south. And a skilled navigator (wayfinder) could work out your latitude (how far north or south you were) by measuring the height of the sun and stars in the sky. Over thousands of years, they developed instruments such as the astrolabe, cross-staff, quadrant and sextant to help them.

But when the sea was rough or clouds obscured the sky, even the most skilled navigators were in trouble, and they could only guess longitude (how far east or west they were) by 'dead reckoning' – that is, by keeping track of your speed to work out how far you had sailed. So the introduction in the Middle Ages of the magnetic compass was a huge breakthrough. It tells you where north is at any time, in any weather. A second key breakthrough was the chronometer, a very accurate clock developed in the 18th century, which enabled sailors to calculate longitude for the first time. But the greatest breakthrough was as recent as 1996 – the satellite system known as GPS (Global Positioning System), which enables all travellers to pinpoint exactly where they are in an instant.

Magnetic north

A compass has a magnetic needle that can swivel freely on a pivot or floating on liquid. The needle always turns to point north, so a sailor can be sure the ship is sailing in the right direction or 'bearing.' The compass was probably invented in China 1,000 years or so ago. By the 1300s, European sailors were relying on compasses, too, and compasses helped European explorers sail out around the world in the 1400s and 1500s. This compass dates from the late 18th century.

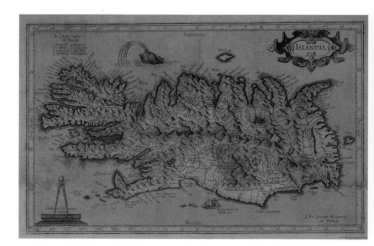

Plotting a course

Because the Earth is round, it is not so easy to plan a long sea journey on a flat map. But in 1569, Flemish mapmaker Gerardus Mercator invented a way of making maps as if the round surface of the Earth was drawn or 'projected' on to the inside of a cylinder. Sailors could plot their course on a Mercator projection map, like this one of Iceland, simply by drawing a straight line to their destination.

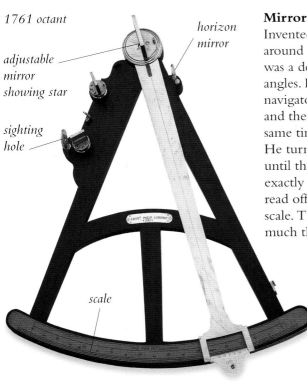

1761 octant

horizon mirror

adjustable mirror showing star

sighting hole

scale

Mirror, mirror…

Invented by John Hadley around 1720, the octant was a device for measuring angles. It allowed the navigator to see both a star and the horizon at the same time in little mirrors. He turned the mirrors until the star and horizon exactly aligned, and then read off the angle on the scale. This worked however much the ship was rocking.

Finding longitude

To work out from the position of the sun exactly how far east or west they had sailed, navigators needed to know the exact time to the minute, many months out at sea. But ordinary pendulum clocks lost time – especially on a rocking ship. In 1761, clockmaker John Harrison managed to make the first 'marine chronometer', a watch that kept perfect time long enough for a ship to cross the Atlantic.

Finding latitude

From the 1460s, navigators often used a simple device called a quadrant to work out latitude. They sighted the Pole Star, or the sun at noon, by looking along one edge. The plumb line (weighted string) hanging down indicated the angle. Markings on the quadrant, adjusted for different times of year, would then indicate the ship's latitude. For example, if the plumb line hangs at 38° when looking at the Pole Star, then the ship is at 38° latitude.

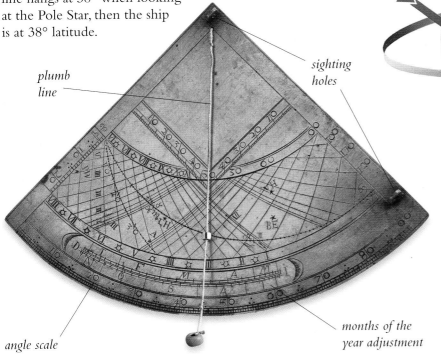

plumb line

sighting holes

angle scale

months of the year adjustment

Global positioning

The Global Positioning System (GPS) is a network of 24 satellites that follow precise orbits around the Earth, each beaming out its own identity signal. Any GPS receiver on Earth, from a smartphone to a ship's onboard navigation computer, can identify its position exactly by comparing the time the signal takes to reach it from the nearest three satellites.

UNDER THE SEA

Drebbel's submarine
This is a modern replica of Drebbel's wooden submarine of 1620. It was like an enclosed rowing boat covered in greased leather to make it watertight. When tested in a lake near London, it dived beneath the surface and rowed underwater for 10 minutes.

LEGEND has it that the Ancient Greek ruler Alexander the Great explored under the sea inside a large glass jar. But the first verified stories of a device to take people underwater come from the 1500s. Many inventors devised 'diving bells' – heavy capsules that are simply lowered into the water with a diver inside. Unlike a submarine, diving bells have no motor, so they can only go straight up and down.

The first submarine was built by Dutchman Cornelius Drebbel for the English navy in 1620. But it wasn't until 1773 that American inventor David Bushnell (1742–1824) made the world's first working submarine, the *Turtle*. Early submarines were all human-powered. Normal engines won't work underwater. So the big breakthrough was the development of battery-powered electric motors, which could drive submarines along underwater. Now there are underwater craft that can stay submerged for months at a time or reach the deepest parts of the ocean. There are even hotels underwater.

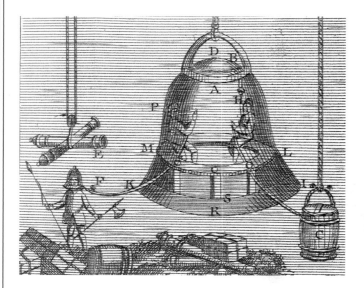

Halley's diving bell
The simplest form of diving bell is just a heavy inverted metal bell shape that is open at the bottom and traps air underneath it. But when the astronomer Edmund Halley created a diving bell in 1691, his design included a number of ingenious improvements, such as a window to let light in at the top. A pipe from the surface and a separate tank supplied the diver with fresh air, while an exhaust let stale air out. Diving bells based on Halley's design were in use for almost 200 years.

Fulton's *Nautilus*
American inventor Robert Fulton created his *Nautilus* in France in the 1790s. With its cigar-shaped copper hull, conning tower, propeller (driven by a hand-crank) and compressed air supply, it was the first practical submarine. It was tested successfully on the River Seine in 1800. It could even outrun a rowing boat. Unfortunately, it leaked and so Fulton could not generate interest to develop it further.

Deep-sea diving

The American research vessel *Alvin*, built in 1964, is a submersible. This means that unlike a submarine, it requires a support crew on the surface. But it can take two scientists and one pilot 4,500m/14,800ft down into the ocean for up to nine hours. It is still in operation after half a century and well over 4,000 dives.

Undersea boat

The famous U-boats were submarines the German navy used to attack Allied shipping in World Wars I and II. Like all modern submarines, U-boats have a double skin. In between the inner skin and the outer skin are large spaces that can hold water, called ballast tanks. To dive, the sub pumps water in to flood these tanks, making the sub heavy enough to sink. To surface, it simply pumps the water out again.

Nuclear secrecy

Modern nuclear submarines are the most secretive craft on Earth. Their nuclear reactors give power to drive their electric motors without any air, and their nuclear fuel is so concentrated that they can go years without refuelling. They can stay submerged for three months, during which time they can travel twice around the world – and they only come up because the crew get hungry…

Scuba diving

With scuba diving equipment, divers can stay underwater for a long time. The first successful scuba system was introduced by Frenchman Jacques Cousteau in 1943. Scuba divers have a tank filled with oxygen under pressure for them to breathe. The oxygen is supplied via a tube to the face mask so the diver can breathe naturally underwater.

STEAM POWER

THE notion of using steam for power dates back over 2,000 years to the Greek inventor Ctesibius, who had an idea for a whirling device using jets of steam from a kettle. But the first steam engine was built in 1698 by English inventor Thomas Savery for pumping water from mines. Savery's engine was prone to blowing up, but in 1712, ironmonger Thomas Newcomen developed a safer design. By the end of the century, steam engines were installed in factories and workshops, mines and mills across Britain – pumping water, running machines and lifting weights.

These early engines were far too heavy to be used for transport. But in 1783, the French nobleman Marquis d'Abbans used one to power a boat up and down the River Saône near Lyons, France. Then in 1804, Cornishman Richard Trevithick mounted his engine on a carriage and set it on a rail track to create the first steam locomotive.

The power of the kettle
Around 250BC, Ctesibius wrote about an 'aeolipile', a kettle that could be made to spin by jets of steam gushing from nozzles. Another Greek inventor, Hero of Alexandria, created a practical design for Ctesibius's aeolipile 350 years later. It worked perfectly.

Dirty old town
The steam engine helped drive the Industrial Revolution, which saw the creation of vast new towns. Noisy, smoky steam-powered factories loomed over packed rows of tiny brick houses – home to tens of thousands of factory workers. The coming of steam railways in the 1830s completed the picture.

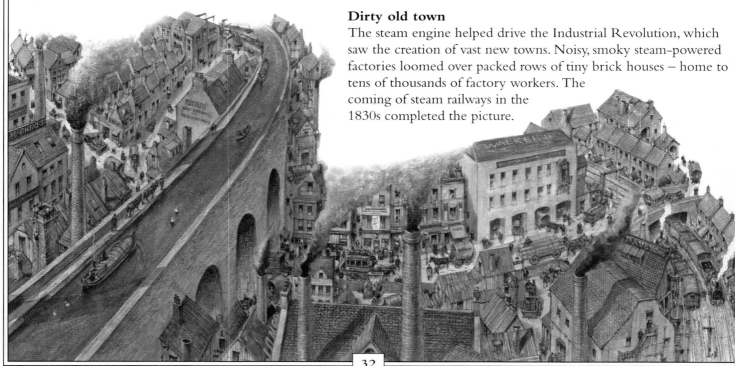

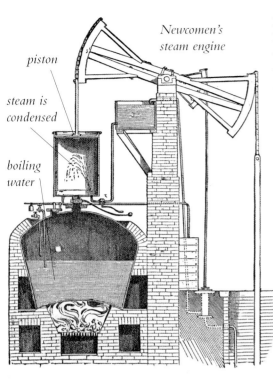

piston

steam is condensed

boiling water

Newcomen's steam engine

Beam me up

Early steam engines were beam engines, in which an arm or beam rocked to and fro to work a pump or run a machine. Newcomen's design was safer than Savery's because it boiled water separately. The steam was piped into the engine's cylinder. There it was cooled to make it condense to water and create a vacuum that pulled on the piston. The steam age really began in 1774 when Scottish engineer James Watt improved the engine's efficiency. Newcomen's design wasted heat by continually chilling the cylinder to condense the steam. So Watt piped the steam out of the cylinder to condense it. Watt's engines were soon being made in huge numbers.

The first steam loco

The low-pressure engines of the 1700s were too cumbersome to drive vehicles. But the powerful little engine invented by Richard Trevithick in 1799 used high-pressure steam. Instead of a vacuum pulling the piston, the steam pressure pushed it. In 1804, Trevithick mounted his engine on a carriage and set it on a rail track to create the first steam locomotive, the *Pen-y-Darren*, named after an ironworks in Wales.

Rocket powered

The world's first public railway opened between Stockton and Darlington in 1825. But the first intercity passenger route was the Liverpool and Manchester Railway (L&MR), which opened in 1830. Trials were held at Rainhill (above) in October 1829 to find the best locomotive to pull L&MR's trains and were famously won by Robert Stephenson's *Rocket*.

Record breaker

Steam locomotives reached their peak in the 1930s and the *Mallard*, designed by Sir Nigel Gresley, was cutting edge technology of the day. On 3rd July 1938, the *Mallard* set the world record speed for a steam locomotive when it hit 203kmh/126mph near Grantham on the line from London to Edinburgh.

MODERN AMENITIES

5,000-year-old loo
In 1850, a great storm in Orkney blew away sand dunes to reveal the stone walls of round houses dating back 5,000 years. They must have been very cosy, with proper cooking areas, cupboards, stone bed bases and even a little room with a toilet!

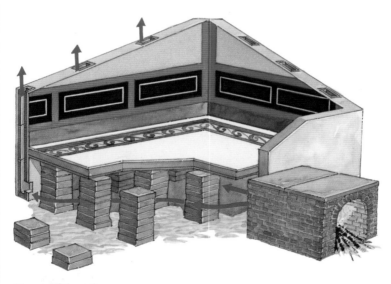

Central heating
The Romans had central heating in the form of the 'hypocaust'. Warm air from a furnace was channelled under the floor and through pipes to warm up buildings. But the idea of piping hot water through ordinary houses to heat them only took off in the late 19th century, after the invention of the radiator by Franz San Galli in chilly St Petersburg around 1855.

What the Romans did for us
The Romans made their cities as comfortable as many modern cities. They used their engineering skills to build 'aqueducts' – channels to supply water. The Pont du Gard bridge in southern France carried the aqueduct that supplied the Roman city of Nemausus (modern Nimes).

OVER thousands of years, people have made many innovations to make living in cities more comfortable and convenient. Imagine having to go out into the wind and rain on a stormy night to go to the toilet. Until quite recently, that's just what many people had to do. Yet archaeologists have found they had indoor flush toilets inside stone cottages 5,000 years ago in the remote village of Skara Brae in the Scottish Orkney Islands. Around the same time, the ancient cities of the Indus Valley Civilization in what is now Pakistan had proper drainage systems, and pipes to supply water to individual houses. The Romans had underfloor heating to warm their houses. They had street lights, too. And yet until the 19th century, most poorer people had to do without all these things, and proper 'central' heating has only become common in the last half century. Until the last century, too, most people lived crammed together in small cottages and houses. Now, many people live in high-rise apartments, and the face of big cities has changed dramatically with the coming of skyscrapers.

Lighting-up time

Modern street lighting started with the invention of the gas lamp by William Murdoch in Redruth, Cornwall in the 1790s. The first gas street lights appeared on Pall Mall in London in 1807. Gas street lights had to be lit by hand every night and they were finally replaced by electric lights in the late 1800s.

Empire State

Two crucial developments gave birth to the modern skyscraper in the late 1800s: the invention of the lift by Elisha Otis in 1857; and the development of steel frames, which meant that even the tallest walls could be very thin. By the 1930s, New York was filled with skyscrapers, of which the tallest was the 443m/1,454ft Empire State Building.

1934 refrigerator

Cool it

In the past, people used ice and caves to keep things such as perishable foods cool, but in 1805 American inventor Oliver Evans realized that things could be refrigerated with compressed gas, which cools when it expands. Florida doctor John Gorrie turned the idea into a reality in the 1840s. The first refrigerator to see widespread use was the General Electric 'Monitor-Top', introduced in 1927. Its compressor assembly was placed on top of the cabinet.

Going underground

Underground railways or 'metros' are now an essential part of getting around modern cities. In the 1800s, people had the idea of firing trains through underground tubes using air pressure. But the first metro was London's Metropolitan line, which opened in 1863, and was just a partly covered cutting with trains pulled by steam engines. Deep tube lines had to wait until the development of electric trains in the 1890s.

ELECTRIC POWER

WITHOUT electricity, the modern world would be very different. We rely on it for everything from running computers and guiding aeroplanes to providing light and heating water. It is one of the basic forces of the universe. The Ancient Greeks knew that rubbing amber creates a strange attraction we now know to be static electricity. But it was only in the 1700s that scientists really began to discover its amazing power and tried to work out how to generate it. In 1752, American statesman Benjamin Franklin proved that lightning is electricity, and in 1800 Alessandro Volta made the first battery. But the breakthrough came in the 1820s, when Michael Faraday in England and Joseph Henry in America discovered how electricity was linked to magnetism. This link led to the invention of generators to make electricity, and electric motors. By 1879, Werner von Siemens had opened the world's first electric railway in Berlin. Just three years later, Thomas Edison was supplying electric power to run electric lights in both London and New York.

Chemical generation
In 1800, Italian scientist Alessandro Volta sandwiched copper and zinc discs and soaked them in salt water. The reaction between the discs created an electric charge. This was the world's first proper battery, soon known as the Voltaic pile, and the first plentiful source of electricity. Here he is showing it to the Emperor Napoleon.

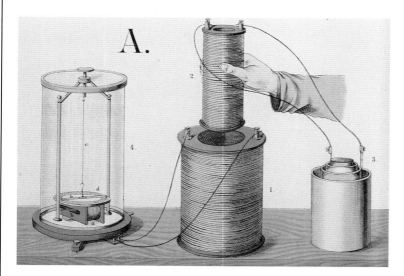

Magnetic generation
In 1831, Faraday and Henry found that when a magnet is moved near an electric circuit, it creates a surge of electricity. This, more than anything, was the discovery that gave us our modern age of electricity, our lights and our computers and TVs. Using this principle, huge machines could be built to generate lots of electricity.

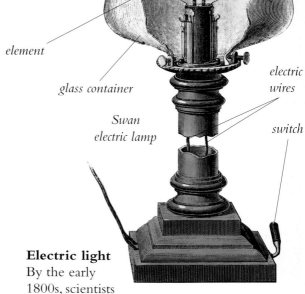

element

glass container

electric wires

Swan electric lamp

switch

Electric light
By the early 1800s, scientists knew that passing electricity through a thin wire could make it heat up and give out light. But it took until the 1870s for Sir Joseph Swan and Thomas Edison to invent light bulbs that would light an ordinary room without quickly burning out. By the 1880s, many homes were lit by electric lamps.

Lighting Venus
One of the first places ever lit by electricity was the Venus Grotto, a cave beneath the Linderhof Castle in Bavaria. Here, in 1878, 24 electricity generators built by Werner von Siemens produced electricity to power 'arc' lamps to shine a blaze of light into the cave. In some ways, the Venus Grotto generators were the first power station.

Nuclear power
Some electricity is made by solar cells, but most is generated by spinning turbines turned by running water (hydro-electric power), the wind or by steam. Some power stations make the heat to create steam by burning coal, oil or gas. In nuclear power stations, the heat comes from nuclear reactions. Unlike coal, oil and gas, nuclear power does not pollute the air, but it creates radiation, which can be dangerous.

Wind power
Burning coal, oil and gas tends to pollute the air, with oxides which make acid rain and carbon dioxide which disrupts the world's climate. In recent years, many countries have tried to develop cleaner ways of generating electricity, such as wind power. Wind turbines like these now generate more than four per cent of the world's electricity.

Hydrogen generation
In the future, more cars may run on hydrogen. The hydrogen is used in a 'fuel cell', which creates electricity like a battery to drive the car's electric motor. The hydrogen fuel combines with oxygen to produce water, so the only emission that comes out of the car's exhaust is pure water.

THE COMING OF THE CAR

THE earliest cars were basically horse carts with an engine instead of a horse. They were even called horseless carriages! The first efforts to create cars used steam engines. As long ago as 1672, a priest called Padre Verbiest designed a model steam car for the Chinese emperor Chien Lung.

In the 1800s, as steam railways took off, many inventors built steam cars, and by 1900 there were thousands of them on the road. But in the end steam engines proved too bulky for cars, because they needed to carry water and coal as fuel. The true future of the car lay with the engine pioneered by Étienne Lenoir in the 1860s. Lenoir's invention was driven by internal combustion – that is, by burning gas inside a cylinder. Lenoir put his engine in a carriage and ran it on petrol rather than gas to create the first petrol-engined car in 1863. It was a petrol engine that powered the first ever car for sale to the public, the Motorwagen of 1888, created by German engineer Karl Benz. Even today, most cars run on petrol.

Cugnot's tricycle

The first full-size steam car was built by French engineer Nicolas-Joseph Cugnot in 1770. It had three wheels and a large copper boiler hanging over the front wheel. It was so heavy it was impossible to steer or stop, and it crashed into a wall!

Trevithick's *Puffing Devil*

Cornish engineer Richard Trevithick, who had built the first steam locomotive, also constructed the first four-wheeled car in 1801. It was called the *Puffing Devil*, because of the clouds of steam that came out of its tall chimney as it chugged through the streets of Camborne in South-West England.

Lenoir's engine

Belgian engineer Étienne Lenoir developed his first internal combustion engine (above) in 1858. It ran on gas made from coal. His key breakthrough was to use an electric spark to ignite the gas. In 1860, he put his engine in a cart, with the engine driving the wheels via a chain. In 1863, he built a three-wheeler with a petrol engine. It was the first real car.

A car to buy

When German engineer Karl Benz built his Motorwagen in 1888, he was not simply attaching an engine to a cart. He wanted to build a motor car – a car for people to buy. His car had only three wheels, but it was a huge success. Within a few years, Benz was selling 600 cars a year. The Benz was soon joined by makes such as Peugeot and Duryea.

On the cheap

Most early cars were hand-built and expensive. But American industrialist Henry Ford wanted to build cars cheap enough for ordinary people to buy them. His answer was the Model T of 1908. The Model T was mass-produced on a factory assembly line, with each worker adding the same part to each car as it slid past. The T was so successful that by the time the last one came out of the factory in 1927, 15 million had been built.

Electric car

In fact, electric cars date back to the 1880s, but recently people have wondered if they could solve the problem of pollution created by petrol and diesel cars. There are now a number of electric cars on the road, such as the Smart Electric Drive. Electric cars are clean, but while a petrol car can be refuelled in minutes, the batteries on an electric car take several hours to recharge.

FACT BOX

- Since 2010, there have been more than 1 billion cars on the road, with over 25% of them in the USA. By 2050, there may well be over 2.5 billion cars.

- The Volkswagen Beetle was the most produced car ever. The first one was made in 1938, and by the time production stopped in 2003, over 21 million Beetles had been built. Volkswagen is German for 'people's car'.

- Most of the world's cars still run on petrol and diesel, and burn up nearly one and a half trillion gallons of oil every year.

Driver, what driver?

An autonomous or driverless car is capable of sensing its environment and navigating without human input. Many such vehicles are being developed. They use a variety of ways to detect their surroundings, including radar, laser light, GPS and computer vision.

FLYING MACHINES

ONCE, people thought the way to fly was to strap on wings and flap like birds. Of course, their attempts mostly ended badly. The first successful flight was made in a balloon, by the French Montgolfier brothers in 1783. The breakthrough for winged aircraft came when Sir George Cayley discovered the special curve that enables a wing to give 'lift'. Cayley built a glider in which his butler made the first manned aeroplane flight in 1849. A year earlier, John Stringfellow and William Henson flew a model plane powered by tiny steam engines for the first powered flight. Over the next half century, inventors experimented with flying machines, some gliders with no power, others propelled by petrol engines and whirling propellers. But they flew only short distances, and could not be steered. The daring hang glider experiments of the German Otto Lilienthal in the 1890s showed how planes might be controlled in the air. Finally, in 1903, the Wright brothers made the first powered, controlled flight.

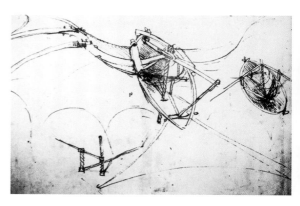

Bird man
The Italian artist and inventor Leonardo da Vinci drew designs for flying machines in the early 1500s. This drawing shows wings that could be strapped to the arms to allow the wearer to fly. However, they were never built.

Flight control
The Americans Orville and Wilbur Wright made their historic flight in their *Flyer* at Kittyhawk, North Carolina on 17th December 1903. Their secret was the way they controlled the flights by pulling cables to change the curve of the wings. In future, planes would control the flight with flaps on the wings, but the Wrights' 'wing-warping' worked.

Whirly bird
Wings provide lift by parting the air as they move forward through it. Helicopter blades whirl around to provide lift without the aircraft needing to move forward. So helicopters can take off and land vertically and hover in the air. The first successful helicopter was built by Russian-born Igor Sikorsky (pictured) in 1940.

Flying boat
The largest commercial aircraft built between World Wars I and II were flying boats of the kind shown here. Because there were few long runways built on land, large planes often took off from, and landed on, water. This six-engined plane flew on routes between Italy and South America.

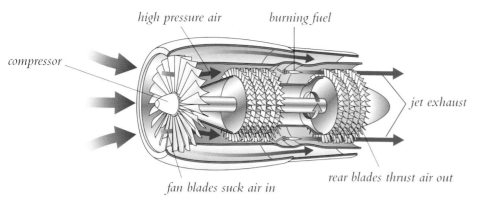

compressor

high pressure air

burning fuel

jet exhaust

fan blades suck air in

rear blades thrust air out

Jet power

From the 1950s, the propellers of early aeroplanes were superseded by the jet engine, developed in the 1930s by Briton Frank Whittle and German Hans von Ohain. Jet engines gulp in air through fan blades that compress the air as they spin, ready to be ignited, and blast the air out the back to drive the plane forward.

Jetsetter

The de Havilland *Comet*, shown here, was the first jet aircraft to go into regular passenger service. It began flying in 1952 and halved the time for long journeys such as that between London and South Africa. Nowadays there are more than 20,000 jet airliners flying people all around the world.

FACT BOX

• The first flight around the world was carried out in 1924 by a team of eight aviators of the United States Army Air Service. The trip took them 175 days, with 74 stops and covering about 44,340km/27,550 miles.

• The first supersonic civilian aircraft to fly was the Russian Tupolev Tu-144 on the last day of 1968.

• The Antonov An-225 *Mriya* is the longest and heaviest plane ever built, with a maximum take-off weight of 640 tons. It also has the largest wingspan of any aircraft in operational service – 88m/290ft.

Stealth craft

By the late 20th century, military jets could fly at breathtaking speeds – three times as fast as sound. The Lockheed SR-71 could cross the Atlantic Ocean in less than two hours. The SR-71 was, like the later F-117A Nighthawk shown here, a 'stealth' plane. It was painted with a special black oxide and carefully shaped to hide it from enemy radar.

Drone delivery

Drones are robot aircraft that fly by remote control. Quadcopters are drones like mini-helicopters with four rotors. They are so small and easy to manoeuvre that they are now being used to deliver parcels directly to your door!

WINGS TO FLY

AIR may look like nothing, but it's full of air particles – and that's why wings work. Wings provide a large area so that enough particles get beneath them to lift them up. But wings have to keep moving air under them to provide the lift. Bird wings do this by flapping, or gliding forward. Aeroplane wings rely on moving fast through the air.

You can see how air gives its support with the first, very simple experiment. Paper is very light, but it is still heavy enough to fall to the ground if you drop it.

A sheet of paper falls more slowly than a ball of paper, but to fly you need wings. In the second experiment, you will see how the difference between a sheet of paper and a wing is a stiff shape and forward movement, by making a paper dart.

AIR SUPPORT
You will need: *sheet of paper.*

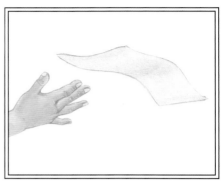

1 Let your sheet of paper go gently and let it drop to the floor.

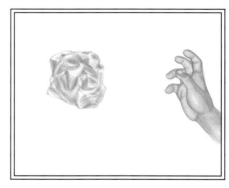

2 Now screw the paper up into as tight a ball as you can, and drop it to the floor again.

You will see that the flat sheet drifts slowly and gently to the ground, while the ball drops quickly and heavily. This is because the sheet has such a large area, it is borne up by a large number of air particles. This is called air resistance. When the paper is screwed into a ball, the weight of the paper is concentrated above far fewer air particles. The air resistance is less, so it falls quickly.

Up in the air
Flying animals and aircraft use moving air to keep themselves airborne. They also have specially shaped wings and a smooth, streamlined body shape.

WING POWER

You will need: *sheet of paper, scissors, sticky tape.*

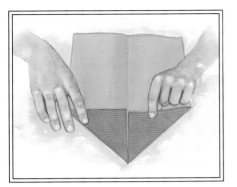

1 Fold a piece of paper down the middle. Open the paper. Fold over the top corners. Make sure they meet in the middle.

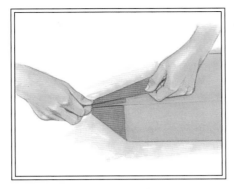

2 Fold the corners of your paper dart into the middle, as shown in the picture.

3 Now fold the sides of the paper into the middle. Cut off the ends using the scissors.

4 Turn the dart over. Fold the sides together. Pull out the sides to make the wings. Tape the top of the wings together.

5 Now hold your dart, slightly nearer the front, and gently throw it forward, launching it on a very slightly upward path.

Why does the dart fly? It flies because your throw gave it the forward momentum to move through the air. The crucial thing is that the weight is concentrated in the heavily folded front. Because the nose slices through the air, the light wings behind move over a lot of air and are borne up.

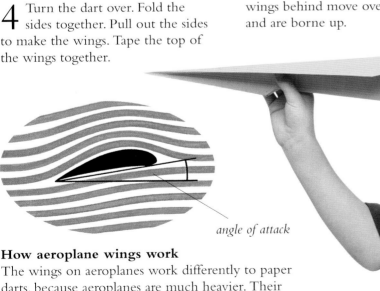

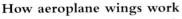
angle of attack

How aeroplane wings work

The wings on aeroplanes work differently to paper darts, because aeroplanes are much heavier. Their wings have a special curved shape or camber, and cut through the air at an angle. This is called the angle of attack. Up to a point, the greater the camber and angle of attack, the greater the lift. The pilot controls the plane by moving flaps on the wing edges to vary the lift each wing gives.

SPACE TRAVEL

I N THE 1890s, a young American boy, Robert Goddard, dreamed of building a machine to carry him to Mars. When he grew up, he devoted his life to creating it. Konstantin Tsiolkovski in Russia and Hermann Oberth in Germany had a similar dream. The answer, they realized, was rockets. Unlike propellers and jets, rockets work in the vacuum of space because they need nothing to push against but the body of the rocket itself. In the 1930s, these three pioneers each developed rockets that could reach high altitudes, and in 1944 German rocket scientist Werner von Braun built a missile rocket, the V2, that flew all the way into space. After World War II, space travel developed amazingly fast. By October 1957, Russia launched the first satellite into space, Sputnik 1, and one month later the Russian space dog Laika became the first animal to orbit the Earth. Two years later, a Russian spacecraft reached the Moon, and in 1961, Russian 'cosmonaut' Yuri Gagarin became the first human in space. Just eight years later, Neil Armstrong and Buzz Aldrin became the first humans to set foot on the Moon.

warhead

alcohol-water mixture (fuel)

liquid oxygen (fuel)

rocket combustion chamber

wing

V2 rocket
The V2 was a German missile rocket that was fired against London from Germany in World War II and killed thousands of people. But on 22nd June 1944, a V2 became the first rocket to travel into space.

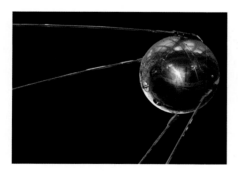

Soviet satellite
Launched on 4th October 1957, Sputnik 1 was the first satellite in space. It took just 98 minutes to complete the first orbit of the Earth. Sputnik is Russian for 'satellite'. Today there are over 500 satellites in space, doing everything from monitoring the state of forests to relaying phone conversations.

Gagarin into space
On 12 April 1961, Yuri Gagarin, in Vostok 1 designed by Sergei Korolev, became the first human in space. Three portholes gave him the first view of Earth from space. He completed one 108-minute orbit of the Earth before Vostok came low enough for him to parachute to safety.

Man on the Moon

In July 1969, the Apollo 11 spacecraft flew three astronauts to an orbit of the Moon. On 20th July, a small landing craft, the *Eagle*, flew down from the Apollo to the surface of the Moon, carrying two astronauts, Neil Armstrong and Buzz Aldrin. Neil Armstrong stepped from the *Eagle* on to the Moon's surface, saying the famous words, "That's one small step for a man, one giant leap for mankind."

Space Shuttle

Most spacecraft can be used only once. But Space Shuttles, although launched on the back of single-use rockets, could come back to Earth and land like a plane, ready for another mission. They were in use from 1981 to 2011.

International Space Station

The ISS was put together bit by bit over dozens of flights as an international project involving Russia, America, Europe, Japan and Canada. Since 2000, it has always had a crew of six, who stay up there for four to six months at a time. It is as big as a football pitch and orbits the Earth at 400km/250 miles above the ground. It zooms around the globe every 90 minutes at a speed of about 28,000kmh/17,500mph.

Space tourism

Up until now, spaceflights have all been government projects and outsiders have only been allowed aboard by special invitation. But a number of businesses are now developing their own spaceplanes for taking paying customers into space. Virgin Galactic's 'SpaceShipTwo' will carry two pilots and six passengers. It could be in operation by 2020. Ticket reservations cost $250,000. Better start saving up!

SEEING MORE

WE CAN see a lot with our own eyes, but by using lenses to make telescopes and microscopes, we can see much more. Lenses bend light rays together and magnify what you see. People knew about lenses over 2,000 years ago, and the 10th-century Muslim scientists Ibn Sahl and Alhazen showed how they worked. Around 1268, the monk Roger Bacon realized that lenses could help people with poor eyesight to see better. Soon, skilled glassmakers were making spectacles. Bacon also suggested that if you put two lenses together you might see the Moon close up.

The telescope is sometimes said to have been invented by the great Italian scientist Galileo (1564–1642). Galileo made the first telescope good enough to see the Moon and planets, in 1609. But he got the idea from novelty telescopes invented a few years earlier by Dutch glassmakers such as Hans Lippershey. The first microscopes appeared at the same time. Then, in the 1660s, Robert Hooke in England and Anton van Leeuwenhoek in Holland – like Galileo with the telescope – developed them for science. Since then, microscopes and telescopes have become ever more powerful. Telescopes can now show us galaxies far across the universe, and microscopes can show us atoms.

Double vision
In the 1700s, Benjamin Franklin, the American statesman, writer and scientist, invented bifocal spectacles. Bifocals are two lenses combined into one. They allow people to see clearly at both short and long distances.

Hooke's look
This is one of the first microscopes, made in the 1660s by English scientist Robert Hooke. Through it, Hooke saw that living things such as the cork in the book are made of tiny 'cells'. A glass globe filled with water helped to focus a bright light. Meanwhile, in Holland, van Leeuwenhoek saw bacteria for the first time through his own simple but powerful microscope.

picture of cork cells

microscope

light focused through globe

Life revealed
Microscopes showed how much of life is invisibly small, from the cells that make up every living thing (including the human body) to tiny organisms such as bacteria. This 19th-century microscope could be used by five medical students at once.

Double barrelled

Binoculars are like two telescopes side by side. They are shorter and less powerful than telescopes but easier to hold in the hand to track things on the move, such as birds in flight. In good binoculars, a pair of prisms (triangles of glass) inside increase magnification by folding the light path double.

Newtonian telescope

Early telescopes using lenses (refracting telescopes) often suffered from coloured blurring. The scientist Isaac Newton realized that this is because light splits into colours as it is refracted (bent) through the edges of lenses. So in 1668 he devised a new kind of telescope (reflecting telescope) which used curved mirrors, not lenses, to focus the light rays. Today most big telescopes for astronomy are reflecting telescopes.

The heavens revealed

It was a powerful moment when Galileo looked through his telescope at the night sky in 1609. Before then, the planets and stars had seemed like little more than patterns in the sky. But the telescope showed that they were worlds every bit as real as our own, just far away. Galileo could see craters on the Moon, and he discovered Jupiter has moons of its own. He also saw that Venus goes through phases like the Moon – which is only possible if the Earth goes around the Sun, which few people had believed before.

FACT BOX

• The largest mirror used in a telescope is the Gran Telescopio Canarias in Spain's Canary Islands. The mirror is over 10m/30ft wide and gives clear views deep into space.

• Electron microscopes allow us to see objects as tiny as atoms. These microscopes do not use lenses but beams of electrons (electrically charged particles).

Deep space

The atmosphere blurs our view of space, so to get a clear view, the Hubble Space Telescope was launched in 1990. It orbits 600km/370 miles above the Earth. It uses very precisely curved mirrors to focus the light from distant galaxies. It has revealed that areas of the sky once thought empty are in fact filled with billions of galaxies far away.

SIMPLE MICROSCOPES

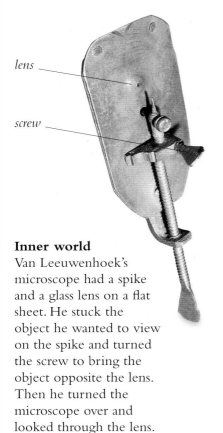

lens

screw

Inner world
Van Leeuwenhoek's microscope had a spike and a glass lens on a flat sheet. He stuck the object he wanted to view on the spike and turned the screw to bring the object opposite the lens. Then he turned the microscope over and looked through the lens.

ONE of the earliest high-powered microscopes was created by Anton van Leeuwenhoek around 1660. Unlike other microscopes, it had just a single lens, which van Leeuwenhoek made by melting a glass rod to make a glass ball the size of a raindrop. It was more like a magnifying glass than a double-lens microscope. But by holding the specimen close to the lens and the lens close to his eye, van Leeuwenhoek was able to achieve magnifications ten times that possible using other microscopes of the time. Whereas other microscopes could magnify by 30 times at most, van Leeuwenhoek's tiny glass ball could give magnifications near 300 times. Such a powerful magnification opened up a world of microscopic life, even in a glass of water.

In the projects on these pages, you can first use glass jars to show how lenses can magnify what we see. Then you can make a microscope like van Leeuwenhoek's by using a tiny droplet of water instead of a glass sphere.

GLASS JAR MICROSCOPE

You will need: *two empty glass jars, water, a pencil.*

1 Fill a glass jar with water and place it at the edge of a table.

2 Look through the jar with one eye and move the pencil back and forth behind the jar. Find the position that gives the clearest image with the greatest magnification.

3 Place a second water-filled glass jar close behind the first one. Hold the pencil in the water in the second jar. Move the pencil back and forth.

4 You will find that the image is about four or five times larger than before.

WATER DROP MAGNIFIER

You will need: *small foil disc (from a drinks bottle, or cut from a sheet of foil), metal spoon (if necessary), candle, small nail, water, flower.*

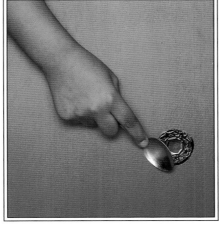

1 Place the foil disc on a hard surface. If necessary, use the outer bowl of a spoon to flatten the foil. Stroke the spoon from side to side until the middle of the foil is flat.

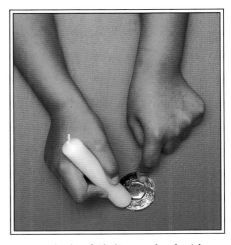

2 Rub the foil disc on both sides with the end of a candle. Make certain that both sides of the smooth middle part are coated with a thin layer of wax.

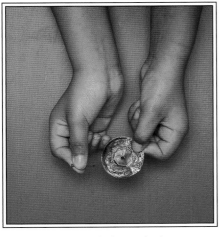

3 Push the nail through the middle of the foil disc to make a small hole in it. The hole should be perfectly round and measure about 2mm/⅛in across.

4 Collect water on a fingertip so that a droplet hangs down. Hold the disc flat and lower the droplet on to the hole. The wax holds the water in a round lens shape.

5 To use your magnifier, hold it about 1–2cm/½–¾in from the object. Now bring your eye as close to the water droplet as possible. Look at how the flower is magnified.

Van Leeuwenhoek's view
Most modern microscopes are large, heavy objects mounted on a bench. But van Leeuwenhoek's microscope is light and can be used by holding it up to the eye. The inventor produced more than 200 of these apparently simple microscopes, and made many discoveries with them, from seeing individual human sperm to bacteria.

TAKING PICTURES

THE world's first photograph was taken less than 200 years ago, but cameras are much older. About 2,500 years ago, Chinese philosopher Mo–Ti saw how light shining through a pinhole in a screen into a darkened room projected a picture of the world outside into the room. In the 1700s, Italian scientist Giovanni Porta added a lens to the pinhole to give a better picture. Artists used rooms like this, called camera obscura (Latin for 'darkened room'), to help create pictures. They soon realized that you could make a portable camera from just a box with a viewing screen at the back. Some began to wonder if they could record the screen image in light-sensitive chemicals. In 1825, Frenchman Joseph Niépce succeeded in creating the world's first (blurred) black and white photos this way. In 1836, another Frenchman, Jacques Daguerre, created the first high-quality photos on metal plates, called daguerreotypes. Meanwhile, Englishman William Fox Talbot created 'calotype' photos on paper which started with a reverse or 'negative' picture. This meant that it could be used to make unlimited copies. With daguerreotypes and calotypes, the age of photography had begun.

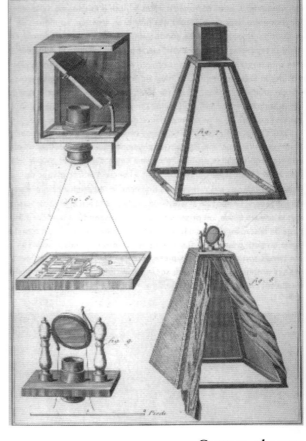

Camera obscura
This portable camera obscura from the 1700s was more like a tent. An angled mirror on top turned the light from the scene at right angles to project the picture through the lens on to the floor of the tent where the artist could draw it.

The world's first photo
This is the world's oldest surviving photo. It was one of several camera obscura pictures recorded by Joseph Nicéphore Niépce on a light-sensitive, bitumen-coated pewter plate. It dates from summer 1826 and was taken in Chalon in France.

Photo portrait
Daguerreotypes were an instant success and soon thousands of wealthy people were going to photographers' studios for a portrait. This one from the 1840s shows English scientist Michael Faraday with his wife Sarah. Each daguerreotype was made on copper coated with light-sensitive silver chemicals and the picture quality is astonishingly good.

And now in colour...

At first, all photos were in black and white. But in 1855, Scottish scientist James Clerk Maxwell suggested a way of making photos in colour by taking three black and white photos, through red, green and blue glass filters. If these were then projected together through the same colour filters, the picture would be in full colour. He and Thomas Sutton made the first colour photo like this, of a tartan ribbon, in 1861.

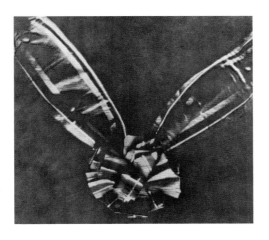

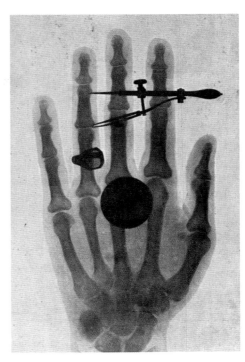

X-ray vision

Photographs have medical uses, too. In 1895, Wilhelm Röntgen noticed that strange 'X'-rays from a cathode ray tube (see page 57) made a nearby screen glow even through a cover. The rays shone through flesh, too, blocked only by bones. Röntgen shone these X-rays through his wife's hand on to photo paper and made the first X-ray photo. He had discovered a new kind of radiation – and a vital way for doctors to see into the body.

Autochrome

Maxwell showed how colour photographs could be made in theory by using three colours, but it wasn't a practical process. The first successful colour photo system was the autochrome, introduced by the French brothers Auguste and Louis Lumière in 1903. The autochome here shows a World War I biplane fighter, in about 1917.

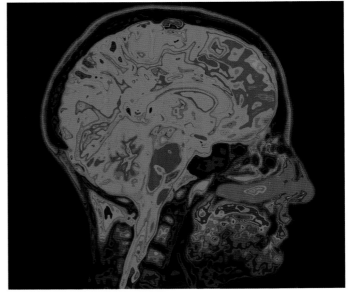

MRI scan

In magnetic resonance imaging (MRI), developed by Paul Lauterbur in 1971, a magnetic field pulls hydrogen particles in the body into alignment. The scanner detects the tiny radio signals the particles send out as they swivel back to normal when the field is switched off.

Digital photography

The light-sensitive pixels in a digital camera can only recognize shades of grey. So a colour filter array (CFA) is placed over them so they record red, green or blue light. The most commonly used pattern in today's CFAs is called the Bayer pattern, after the Kodak technician who invented it.

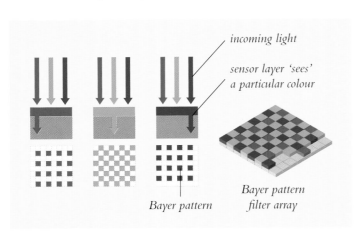

incoming light

sensor layer 'sees' a particular colour

Bayer pattern

Bayer pattern filter array

RECORDING SOUNDS

TODAY'S smartphones can give you almost any music you want, anywhere you want. It all depends on electronics. But the first recording devices all worked mechanically. They captured sounds by funnelling them into a big horn to make the vibrations move a needle directly to engrave scratches on a disc or cylinder. This was how, in 1860, French bookseller Édouard-Léon Scott de Martinville made the oldest known recording of a human voice, and how, in 1877, Thomas Edison created the phonograph, the first device for recording and playing back sounds. But the same year that he launched his phonograph, Edison, along with David Hughes and Emile Berliner, independently invented the microphone. Microphones turn sound vibrations into a varying electrical signal. At first, they were used only for telephones. But by the 1920s they had replaced mechanical horns, and sound recording became electrical. Even so, the electrical signals were stored for playback mechanically in the grooves of shellac and later plastic 'vinyl' records. It wasn't until recently that mechanical storage disappeared entirely with the coming of the electronic digital storage we are now so familiar with.

The oldest known recording
On 9th April 1860, de Martinville recorded someone singing in the scratches on the carbon cylinder on his phonautograph. His machine wasn't designed for playback, just using a moving needle to draw a graphic showing the notes. But in 2008, sound scientists used computers to bring to life the crackly sound of the song, 'Clair de la Lune,' re-creating the oldest known recording of the human voice.

Mechanical sound recording
Edison's phonograph of 1877 was the first device able to play back as well as record sound. The sound was funnelled down a big horn to shake a needle and recorded the sound as grooves in a foil-covered cylinder. By 1909, you could buy professional wax-cylinder recordings to play by turning the handle.

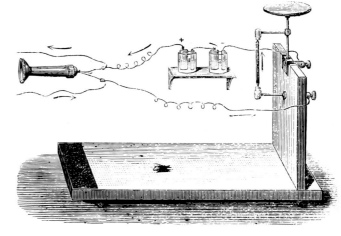

Electrical sound recording
In the 1870s, Thomas Edison, David Hughes and Emile Berliner independently invented the microphone for turning sound vibrations into a varying electrical signal. Microphones were first used only for telephones, but from the 1920s they rapidly replaced the crackly mechanical recordings made by horns for sound recording, too. The improvement in quality was dramatic and the 'talkies' arrived in the movies with a bang.

Playing around

Edison's phonograph cylinders could only be copied a few times. But in 1888, the problem was solved by Berliner's gramophone discs, made from a resin called shellac. Discs could be copied numerous times without any loss of quality. As you played the record, the needle followed a spiral groove responding to all the tiny bumps in which the music was recorded. In 1947, shellac discs were replaced by long-playing vinyl records.

Moog music

Loudspeakers re-create a recorded sound from an electrical signal. But in the 1920s, inventors realized you could use an electric signal to create or 'synthesize' an entirely new sound. With the invention of the transistor, synthesizers such as the Moog became compact enough to use on stage to create weird and wonderful sounds.

Analogue v digital

In 1982, with the arrival of compact disc or CD, music started to go 'digital'. Previously music was 'analogue', in which the electrical signal varies with the shape of the sound wave. In digital sound, the recording is broken into a series of snapshots of the sound. CDs are plastic discs that store the sound digitally in tiny pits that can be read by a laser.

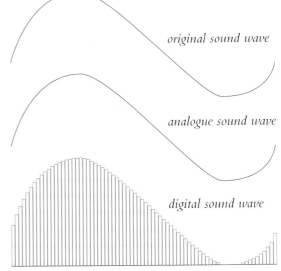

original sound wave

analogue sound wave

digital sound wave

Instant music

By 2001, you no longer needed to store music separately on a CD, record or tape. It could all be stored electronically in a computer's memory, in a digital audio format such as MP3. Apple's iPod took digital music one step further, storing your entire music library in a device no bigger than a matchbox. Now, of course, you can instantly download any music you want from the internet, or stream it 'live' to your music player.

SENDING SOUNDS

Nowadays, you can talk instantly to someone on the other side of the world. It all began with the invention of the electric telegraph around 1844. With the telegraph you could send messages instantly for the first time along a wire, by switching the current on in a code devised by Samuel Morse. Not long after, in 1861, young German Philip Reis had the idea that if you turned sounds into an electric signal, you could send speech by wire, too. Scottish-born inventor Alexander Graham Bell turned Reis's idea into reality in 1876 and launched the telephone. A decade later, another young German, Heinrich Hertz, showed how an electric spark sends out invisible waves that could generate an electric current in a 'receiver'. Brilliant Italian inventor Guglielmo Marconi instantly realized how these 'radio' waves could be used to transmit sound signals through the air, without even a wire. Mobile phones transmit messages in the same way, using microwaves rather than radio waves.

Wire code
The telegraph was invented independently by Samuel Morse in the USA and William Cooke and Charles Wheatstone in England. To send a message, the telegraph operator used a simple spring-loaded switch to turn the current on for a short time (a dot) or a longer one (a dash). Letters were represented by a code of three dots or dashes.

Transatlantic message
In 1858, the first telegraph cable right under the Atlantic Ocean was completed. This meant that messages which had previously taken ten days to send by ship could now be transmitted in a matter of minutes. The first message, sent from England on 16th August 1858, was: "Europe and America are united by telegraphy. Glory to God in the highest; on earth, peace and good will toward men."

The transatlantic cable arriving at Heart's Content in Newfoundland.

1924 telephone

First call
On 10th March 1876, Alexander Graham Bell made the world's first phone call, to Thomas Watson, the electrical engineer who was helping him with his experiments. Watson was in another room in Bell's house in Boston, USA, and Bell said just, "Mr Watson, come here. I want to see you."

Radio signal

In 1901, Guglielmo Marconi travelled to Newfoundland in Canada to prove just how amazing his new invention of radio was by receiving the first transatlantic radio message. Some people had said it would not work, since the radio signal could not be picked up beyond the horizon. In fact, it bounced off the atmosphere right across the ocean more than 3,000km/2,000 miles from Poldhu in Cornwall, England, to Newfoundland.

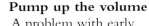

an early transistor radio

Pump up the volume

A problem with early radio was making the sound loud enough to hear. That's why the invention of the triode by American inventor Lee de Forest in 1906 was a breakthrough. The triode used the electrical signal to control a much bigger current, amplifying it. However, triodes consumed a lot of power and broke easily. Then in 1947, John Bardeen, Walter Brattain and William Shockley at AT&T's Bell Labs in the USA created the transistor. This uses the changing electrical resistance of certain substances to create the same effect as the triode but is much smaller and harder to break. Soon, compact and portable transistor radios were in use in millions of homes.

Telstar

The launch of the Telstar 1 satellite in July 1962 was the beginning of a new era in telecommunications. Instead of relying on long cables overground or under the ocean, telephone calls could be beamed up to satellites as microwaves and bounced instantly to the other side of the world. Now most international calls go via satellite.

The evolution of the mobile phone, from left to right: Motorola 8900X-2 (a 1994 'brick' phone), Nokia 2146, Nokia 3210, Nokia 3510, Nokia 6210, Ericsson T39, HTC Typhoon (an early smartphone), 1st generation iPhone.

Wireless phones

The idea of wireless telephones dates back to 1908. But the first mobile phone call was made by Motorola engineer Martin Cooper on 3rd April 1973. That first mobile was gigantic and weighed ten times as much as today's smartphones. Yet today's smartphones contain as much computer processing power as the computers that guided spacecraft to the Moon in the 1960s. Early mobile phones were called cell phones, because the signal was divided into cell-like zones around each transmitting mast.

MOVING PICTURES

BACK in the 19th century, scientists discovered that light can trigger electric currents. They soon developed photocells that sent an electrical signal when they detected light. In the 1880s, German inventor Paul Nipkow had the idea that you could scan the light from a whole scene and create a moving picture by putting a rapidly spinning disc with a spiral of holes in front of a photocell.

In the meantime, in the 1890s, Guglielmo Marconi invented radio. This works by turning sounds into an electrical signal, then using the signal to beam out invisible radio waves. A receiver turns the radio waves back into an electrical signal to re-create the sound.

In 1926, Scottish inventor John Logie Baird succeeded in using Nipkow's spinning disc system to broadcast live, moving pictures for the first time. Baird's mechanical system worked, but the picture it produced was poor. The future lay with the electronic system developed by Russian engineer Vladimir Zworykin. His system used a cathode ray to scan to and fro to build up the picture. By the 1950s, televisions based on cathode ray tubes were appearing in homes across the world.

Horse in motion
In 1877, a horse trainer asked English photographer Eadweard Muybridge to prove for a bet that all four legs of a galloping horse come off the ground at some point. Muybridge captured a complete sequence of the horse in motion by setting up 50 cameras along the track and firing them electrically as the horse passed. Muybridge won the trainer his bet, and laid the foundations of moving pictures.

cinématographe

The movies
By 1893, Thomas Edison had invented a camera to record moving pictures, and a 'kinetoscope' to show them. However, only one person could look into the kinetoscope at a time. Then in 1895, Auguste and Louis Lumière created the cinématographe (pictured here), which projected moving pictures on to a screen for all to see.

dummy head used in Baird's tests — *spinning discs* — *electric motor*

In a spin

Baird used Nipkow's mechanical spinning disc system to create the first television broadcast in 1926. Two years later, he made the first transatlantic TV broadcast. The discs had to spin so quickly that they were quite dangerous! When the BBC began broadcasting TV in the 1930s, they used Baird's system, but soon switched to the electronic system, which gave a better picture.

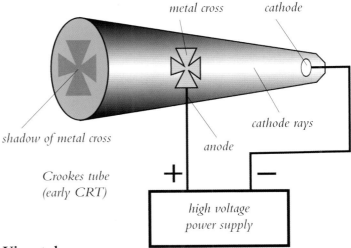

metal cross — *cathode* — *shadow of metal cross* — *anode* — *cathode rays* — *Crookes tube (early CRT)* — + — − — *high voltage power supply*

View tube

Photocells turn pictures into an electric signal; and, until recently, a cathode ray tube (CRT) turned the signal back into a picture. Cathode rays were discovered in the 1860s when scientists saw a green glow as electricity zapped between two electric terminals in a vacuum-filled glass tube. The glow was rays from the cathode (negative terminal). In a TV with a CRT, magnets steer the rays to draw the glowing picture on the screen. Since the late 2000s, CRTs have been mostly replaced by newer, slimmer technologies such as liquid crystal display (LCD), light emitting diodes (LED) and plasma display.

Light entertainment

In 1839, French physicist Edmond Becquerel, aged just 19, noticed that if he shone light on electrodes (electric terminals) dipped in chemical solution, the electric current increased. He'd made the first ever photocell – a cell that gives an electric current when exposed to light. Photocells made TV cameras possible, turning the light making up a scene into an electric signal, which can then be displayed on a TV screen. This is a black and white set from the 1950s.

ARTIFICIAL INTELLIGENCE

THE origins of the computer date back 5,000 years to when people in Asia used abacuses to help with sums. An abacus is a simple frame with rows of sliding beads, but a skilled user can use it to do tricky sums very quickly. In the 1600s, mathematicians made adding machines with gears and dials. But the idea of computing started with the 'analytic engine' designed by English inventor Charles Babbage in the 1830s. It was never built, but it introduced the idea of programming, using cards punched with holes to control the movement of its rods and gears. But mechanical rods and gears were just too awkward for a full-scale computer, and the breakthrough came in World War II in the machine developed by English mathematician Alan Turing to break secret enemy codes. It was called Colossus, it used electronic valves rather than rods and gears, and was the first real computer.

Making it count
People have been using this kind of counting device for thousands of years. It is known in Chinese as a *suan pan* and as an abacus in English. Beads are arranged on vertical, parallel rods. Each rod represents different kinds of number. For example, on the extreme left are 1s, next left 10s. By sliding the beads up and down, a person can quickly perform complicated arithmetic.

Making a difference
Before he developed the idea for the analytic engine, Babbage tried to build a machine he called the difference engine. The analytic engine would have been the first computer, a machine that could respond to problems and solve them by itself. The difference engine was just a clever calculator. But even this was so complicated to make with metal rods and gears that Babbage finished only part of it.

Codebreaker
Colossus was the pioneering computer developed by Turing in World War II to break secret 'Enigma' codes used by the Germans. Rather than metal gears, Colossus used electronic valves to control the rapid switching between paths as it made its calculations. It also incorporated many of the basic rules that computer programs rely on today.

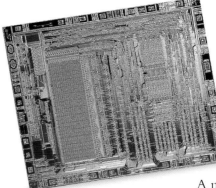

Silicon chip

Today's computers are much smaller than the first computers thanks to microchips, pioneered by American engineer Jack Kilby in 1957. A microchip is a tiny but complicated network of electronic circuits printed onto a small piece or 'chip' of silicon. It works very hard, so gets very hot, which is why a computer needs to have a fan running all the time.

World Wide Web

Tim Berners-Lee revolutionized the way in which the world communicates, with his invention of the World Wide Web in 1990. The internet dates back to the 1960s, but it was all rather inaccessible. The World Wide Web transformed computer output into simple web pages that could be read and displayed by any computer accessing the internet, anywhere in the world.

Tablet computer

In the 1968 science fiction film *2001: A Space Odyssey*, astronauts were shown using tablet computers – and sure enough, by 2001, there were tablet computers available. But the breakthrough for tablets was the introduction of the Apple iPad in 2010, with its neat design and touch-screen operation.

Rise of the robots

Mechanical moving figures, called automatons, date back thousands of years. But computer technology has created the possibility of robots, machines that can do complex tasks by themselves, and respond to changes. Machines like these are used in everything from building cars to exploring volcanoes. But the dream of many designers is to create a robot that's just like a human. Aldebaran Robotics' Nao robots are among the first to be partially self-aware.

THROUGH THE LOGIC GATE

INFORMATION flowing inside a computer is called data. It is in the form of electrical pulses. Data changes as it passes through part of the computer called the central processing unit (CPU). The CPU has thousands of separate high-speed switches called logic gates. These logic gates are microscopic transistors cut into a silicon chip. They can flick on and off up to 300 million times per second. Data flows into the input side of each gate. It only flows out again if the gate is switched on. The computer program sets up how the gates switch on and off and so controls the data flow through the computer.

There are three main types of gates, called AND, NOT and OR gates. Working together, they act as counters or memory circuits to store data. Logic gates are also used to control things like washing machines. In this project, you can make two model logic gates to show how the output depends on the settings of the two input connections.

AND gate	A B	C
Input A	Input B	Output C
OFF	OFF	OFF
OFF	ON	OFF
ON	OFF	OFF
ON	ON	ON

OR gate	A B	C
Input A	Input B	Output C
OFF	OFF	OFF
OFF	ON	ON
ON	OFF	ON
ON	ON	ON

On or off?
AND and OR gates both have two input (A and B) and one output connection (C). The tables above show how the ON/OFF states of the inputs affect the ON/OFF state of the output. These tables are called 'truth tables'.

MAKE A LOGIC GATE

You will need: felt-tipped pen, ruler, stiff card in dark blue, light blue and yellow, scissors, stapler, pencil, small red and green circle stickers.

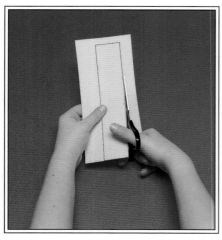

1 Mark and cut out four pieces of card in the following sizes: 15 x 10cm/6 x 4in (dark blue), 10 x 7cm/ 4 x 3½in (light blue) and two of 4 x 20cm/1½ x 8in (yellow).

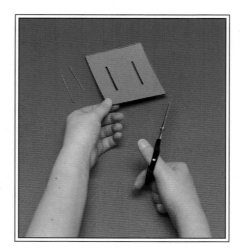

2 On the light blue card, draw two slots that are slightly more than 4cm/1½in wide and 4cm/1½in apart. Cut each slot so that it is about 2–3mm/1/16–1/8in wide.

3 Place the card with slots in the middle of the dark blue card. Staple them together with one staple at each corner of the top card. Draw the three arrows as shown.

4 At 2cm/¾in intervals, stick red and green circles in the order shown on to the left side of a long card strip. This is the input side. Red means OFF and green means ON.

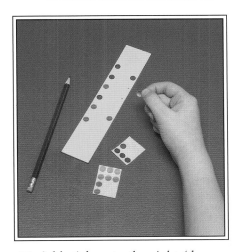

5 Add stickers to the right (the output side) at 2cm/¾in intervals, in the order green, green, green, green, red. Each sticker should be halfway between two on the left.

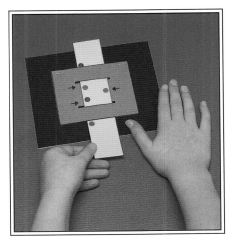

6 Now make a similar strip, but with the stickers on the right in the order green, red, red, red, red. Push this strip between the two stapled cards and through the slots.

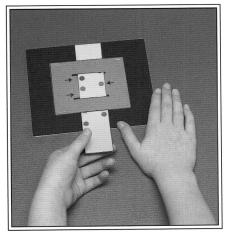

7 Move the strip until there is one green dot and one red dot on the input side. There will be a red dot on the output side. Your model is showing that when only one input is ON, the output is OFF.

8 Only when both dots on the input side are green will a green dot appear on the output side. This shows that both inputs must be ON for the output to be ON. This is how an AND gate works.

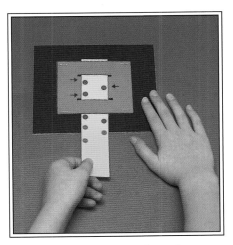

9 Now try inserting the other strip. This one is an OR gate. Notice how it works. You will find that it behaves very differently to an AND gate.

completed model OR gate

10 With the OR gate, the output is OFF only when both inputs are OFF. All other combinations of input will turn the output ON. With the AND gate, both inputs needed to be ON, and all other combinations of input turned the output OFF.

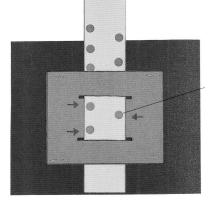

red output indicates that both inputs are OFF

GLOSSARY

anaesthetic
Substance used to numb pain while a doctor operates.

anatomy
The physical layout of the body.

angle of attack
The angle at which a wing cuts through the air.

antiseptic
A substance that keeps things clean from germs.

aqueduct
A channel carrying drinking water, or a bridge carrying a canal.

astrolabe
A disc with dials for calculating the movements of the sun, moon, planets and stars.

blast furnace
A furnace in which air is blown in to create high temperatures to make iron on a large scale.

bow drill
A stick spun at speed with a bow moved to and fro very quickly to light a fire.

bronze
An early discovered alloy (combination) of tin and copper.

cable-stayed bridge
A bridge supported by cables attached directly to a tower.

camera obscura
A darkened room or a box with a lens that projects a picture of the world into the inside.

cantilever
A projecting beam supported only at one end.

casting
Shaping metal by melting it and pouring it into a mould or cast to cool and set solid.

cathode ray tube
A glass tube emptied of air in which the electric charge buzzing from a cathode (a positive electrical terminal) produces a glow.

chemical reaction
Changes that happen when certain chemicals meet certain other chemicals.

chronometer
A highly accurate clock used by sailors to help them calculate their longitude – how far east or west they are.

clipper
A very light, fast sailing ship with a vast sail area used in the mid-1800s to race tea from China to London.

compass
A simple direction-finding device containing a magnetic needle that swivels to point north.

composite material
Material made by combining two materials with different qualities.

diving bell
A device shaped like a bell that traps air inside so it can be lowered into the water with a person inside it.

drone
A small computer-controlled flying machine – typically with four small rotors, like a helicopter.

electrolysis
A process in which certain substances are broken into simpler substances when an electric current is passed through them.

fuel cell
A device that converts chemical energy into electricity using fuels such as hydrogen.

hand drill
A stick spun very quickly between the hands to light a fire.

hydro-electric power
Electric power generated by falling or flowing water.

internal combustion engine
Engine that gets its power by burning fuel, typically petrol, inside a cylinder.

kinetoscope
An early device for viewing moving pictures.

lateen sail
A triangular sail running along the length of a boat.

latitude
How far north or south you are on the Earth, determined by the angle made between you, the centre of the Earth and the equator.

longitude
How far east or west you are, determined by the angle made between you, the centre of the Earth and the prime meridian, a line of longitude that runs through Greenwich, London.

loom
A frame for weaving threads into cloth.

magnetic north
The spot near the North Pole to which all magnetic compasses point.

microchip
A tiny set of complete electronic components and circuits on a single chip of silicon.

mill
Originally a building for grinding corn, but later a factory powered by water.

pendulum
A weight hanging from a support so that it swings freely back and forth under the influence of gravity.

phonograph
A device invented in 1877 for mechanically recording and playing back sounds.

photocell
An electronic device that converts light into electricity.

piston
A drum shape that moves up and down inside a snug-fitting cylinder as it is pushed by liquid or gas.

polymer
A long chemical molecule, such as various plastics, made from clusters of molecules linked together.

quadrant
An instrument used for measuring the angle of stars in the sky in astronomy and navigation.

quern
Stone for grinding cereal crops.

reflecting telescope
A telescope that uses curved mirrors to magnify the picture. Also called a Newtonian telescope.

refracting telescope
A telescope that uses lenses to magnify the picture. Also called a Galilean telescope.

sextant
An instrument used for measuring the angle of stars in the sky in astronomy and navigation, with a double viewer for taking measurements on a moving boat more easily.

smallpox
An often deadly disease that causes the victim's body to erupt in spots or 'pox' – now thankfully eradicated.

spinning wheel
A wheel used to spin threads together from natural fibres.

stethoscope
A medical instrument used for listening to someone's heart or breathing.

submersible
A small boat used for underwater exploration.

suspension bridge
A bridge hung from cables slung between towers on either side.

telegraph
A system that uses electrical signals to send messages, usually carried by telephone lines or radio.

transistor
A tiny solid device that is used to amplify or switch electronic signals and electrical power.

trireme
A warship of Ancient Greece propelled by three rows of oarsmen.

turbine
A machine in which a fan blade turned by steam or water produces continuous power.

vaccination
When people are protected against disease by the injection of a harmless variety of the germ to boost their natural immunity.

valve
In electronics, a device in which a special glass tube, also known as a vacuum tube, controls or amplifies an electric current.

water frame
An industrial spinning machine powered by water.

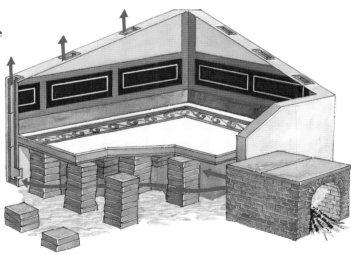

INDEX